The Encyclopedia of
SCRAPBOOKING
TECHNIQUES

A step-by-step guide to creating beautiful scrapbook pages

KAREN McIVOR
AND
SARAH MASON

SEARCH PRESS

A QUARTO BOOK

Published in paperback in 2006 by Search Press Ltd
Wellwood
North Farm Road
Tunbridge Wells
Kent TN2 3DR
United Kingdom
www.searchpress.com

ISBN-13: 978-1-84448-062-3
ISBN-10: 1-84448-062-3

Conceived, designed and produced by
Quarto Publishing plc
The Old Brewery
6 Blundell Street
London N7 9BH

QUAR.ESBT

Project Editor: Mary Groom
Art Editor: Claire van Rhyn
Assistant Art Director: Penny Cobb
Designer: Andrew Easton
Copy Editor: Bridget Jones
Photographers: Paul Forester, Lizzie Orme
Illustrator: Kuo Kang Chen
Picture Research: Claudia Tate

Art Director: Moira Clinch
Publisher: Paul Carslake

Manufactured by Universal Graphics PTE Ltd, Singapore
Printed by SNP Leefung Printer Limited, China

CONTENTS

INTRODUCTION

The craft of scrapbooking is not new – in fact, it has been around for as long as there has been photography. The desire to record personal stories together with images that bring them to life is as strong now as it was over 100 years ago. Most of us have drawers, boxes or bags full of photographs that hold precious memories. Scrapbooking provides the opportunity to preserve these memories, both literally through the use of archival products and by taking the time to record our stories and memories for future generations.

Scrapbooking is also a wonderful creative outlet, drawing upon the skills and techniques used in a host of other crafts. Unlike many other craft products, scrapbook pages are made to be treasured and preserved for years, creating heirlooms that can be inherited and passed on. We hope that the skills and techniques you will find here will inspire and excite you to create pages and albums to treasure.

About this book

Scrapbook principles

The first part of the book explores the fundamental principles of scrapbooking – how to take and use photographs to best effect and how to use composition and design principles to create exciting layouts. Advice and suggestions for journaling – the preservation of your own thoughts and memories – are also included, along with practical examples.

Techniques

The second part of the book focuses on key scrapbooking techniques. Each technique is accompanied by detailed step-by-step instructions, so you can follow the procedure at each stage, and finished examples, which show the techniques in the context of professionally produced scrapbook pages.

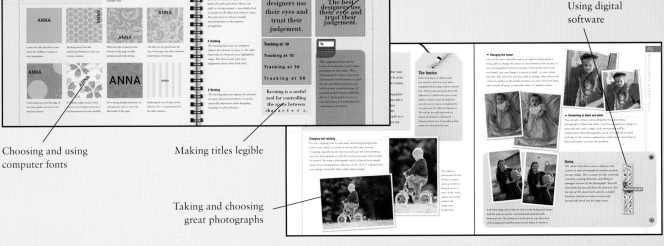

Creating dynamic titles
and positioning words

Using digital
software

Choosing and using
computer fonts

Making titles legible

Taking and choosing
great photographs

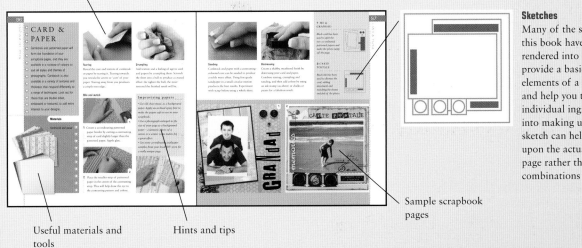

Step-by-step photographs

Sketches

Many of the scrapbook pages in
this book have also been
rendered into a sketch. Sketches
provide a basic map of the
elements of a scrapbook page
and help you to understand the
individual ingredients that go
into making up the page. A
sketch can help you to focus
upon the actual design of the
page rather than specific colour
combinations or photographs.

Sample scrapbook
pages

Useful materials and
tools

Hints and tips

CHAPTER 1

THE PRINCIPLES OF SCRAPBOOKING

Focusing on a practical starting point is important when scrapbooking, particularly when faced with a large pile of photographs – every one a favourite. The many different products now available to create and enhance pages offer so much choice that they can be overwhelming, and it can be difficult to know where to start. In this section, you will be guided through some of the basic principles of scrapbooking to help simplify the process and keep you on the right track. You will be offered advice and tips on selecting the appropriate photographs for your scrapbook pages, and how to store them in the best conditions to prolong their life. Beginning by selecting an appropriate theme for each page, you can learn how to highlight the events and emotions captured in pictures that make scrapbooks more meaningful than straightforward photograph albums.

CHOOSING A THEME

The theme of your scrapbooking page is conveyed and reinforced through every element you see on the layout – photographs, lettering, papers, embellishments. To come up with a theme, start by looking at your photographs.

ONE PICTURE, MANY THEMES

Themes may seem obvious in some cases – if it's a picture of someone's birthday, use birthday embellishments; if it's Christmas then use seasonal accents – but it's not always that easy. What about those photographs that don't really have a theme, or that have many possible themes? Remember that it can be both fun and challenging to try to tackle slightly less obvious themes.

▶ Themes mean memories

The main subject of this photograph is the child's first time flying a kite, but this is not the only possible theme. Themes could also include the family's day out in the park. The important point is to select a theme that is meaningful to you, and brings out a personal aspect of the situation or subject.

▼ Sharing and caring themes

The theme for this photo could simply be 'bubbles'. You could find fun embellishments and lettering to complement the main picture. Alternatively, the theme could be 'sharing' or 'friendship' – and other photographs of the two friends could be used alongside this one.

▶ Events as themes

'The school play' is the first theme that comes to mind with this photograph. But it could also be part of a page about school activities. It may be representative of a newly discovered talent or a key stage in growing up. Photographs on the same theme can be collected over years – showing growing talent or developing skills.

Some themes to get you started

- Home sweet home
- Brotherly love
- Graduation day
- First day at camp
- Gone fishin'
- Seaside fun
- Wedding day
- Day at the zoo
- Grandma

TAKING INSPIRATION FROM YOUR PHOTOS

Inspiration for a theme can come from many elements within the composition or image.

Looking at the age of the people present in your photographs may give you a place to start. There are a host of different patterned papers that are appropriate to different age groups – from bright and colourful for children and fresh and funky for teens to soft and muted for older age groups.

Sometimes the colour of the photograph itself will determine the theme. A strong colour, such as the green of a tree, can affect the theme and colouring of your page. For pictures that contain a lot of different colours, you could consider changing the photograph to black and white. This can help to establish what the main focal point of the picture is by removing the distractions of colour and also makes the photograph easier to use with other colours in your theme.

The era when the photograph was taken may also help to inspire you. Pictures from the 50s, 60s and 70s, for example, will all have a very different look and you can match this with appropriate themed papers or other products that can really emphasise the focus of your pictures.

Creating your theme

▲ Heritage

Very old photographs work best when used with heritage-themed products. Soft, subdued background papers and matching embellishments, such as metal plaques or lace fabric, complement the age and feel of the photos. Muted colours or monochrome schemes work particularly well with old sepia photographs.

A personal approach

Another option is to look outside of the photograph itself and instead consider your personal thoughts and feelings as a theme. What does the subject of the picture mean to you? How does it make you feel? As a theme, try to convery your response, and select tones of colour that complement these feelings.

In this scrapbook page (right) the warm, muted colours of the background papers were chosen to reflect the scrapbooker's feelings about the photo, as well as complementing the colours in the photograph itself.

friends forever

▶ Retro

Photographs from a few decades ago look great when matched with retro-themed products. These often come in colours and patterns which complement the fashions and backgrounds of the photos. Choose the embellishments with care to achieve fun, retro pages.

◀ Modern

Modern-day photographs have a bright, glossy look that works particularly well when matched with modern-themed products. The wide range of styles and colours now available means that you are sure to find something suitable. Don't be afraid to experiment with unusual combinations – they can often lead to the most pleasing effects.

Try working backwards

An unusual way to begin creating a page is to take embellishments and patterned papers as your inspiration and from there, choose photographs to fit. It is a different method of working but it can lead to some fun and interesting pages.

In this example, the inspiration for the theme came from the pink baby-themed paper, co-ordinating cardstock stickers and soft sheer pink ribbon. Suitable photos were then found to match.

GET ORGANISED

Organisation is the key to using your time and resources effectively and this is particularly true when it comes to scrapbooking, which can require a lot of supplies and tools. Being organised is the key to keeping track of what you have, and where you have it.

The easiest way to organise your creative materials is to group items of similar types together – templates in one place, papers and cardstock in another, and so on. Organising by type will help you to determine your storage requirements – do you need storage for lots of small embellishments, or do you need larger storage containers for tools and cardstock?

Safely storing your photographs and other memorabilia ready for scrapbooking is as important as any other archiving aspect of scrapbooking. Photographs are a precious record of lives and the very essence of scrapbooking is learning to preserve your photographs for future generations.

▼ Storing embellishments

There are a number of different systems available to store embellishments, including compartmentalised boxes and stacking containers. Small compartments inside multiple containers provide space for separating groups of items by colour or size. Look for containers that allow you to view the contents, as this will save time and effort when you are tracking down the perfect embellishment for your project.

▲ Scrapbooking on the move

With special storage carrybags, your scrapbooking supplies can travel with you to where your memories are made.

▼ Photo storage systems

Look for storage systems that are acid free. There are a number of systems available, from photo storage boxes and envelopes to accordion, or concertina, files. These are all specifically designed to protect and preserve photographs, and are also ideal for printed memorabilia.

▲ Storing digital images

It is equally important to archive digital images. Computers can crash, hard drives can fail, or disks can be damaged, and all may result in the loss of precious images. Archive copies of files on disc or external computer drives; alternatively, store your pictures on the internet – there are websites that allow you to upload photos, ready to be retrieved at any time.

▶ Protecting photographs

To protect your pictures, store them in PVC-free sleeves that will minimise handling and reduce the risk of physical deterioration and chemical damage from the acid naturally occurring in skin. Store the sleeves in binders or boxes for quick and easy access.

▶ Labelling

Labelling your storage boxes, photos and other supplies clearly by category means you will be able to find and refer to the contents quickly and easily in the future.

SELECTING YOUR PHOTOGRAPHS

The focal point of your scrapbook pages will be your photographs, so selecting the right pictures to scrapbook is a key factor in creating beautiful albums full of memories.

The first step is to sort and organise your existing photographs so that you will be able to find the right one when you want it. There are many different systems, but the practical option is to sort photographs chronologically – by date – or by theme, as both allow additional pictures to be added later. Remember that not all photographs will have a specific theme, so filing them in date order means you will have a place for every item, regardless of content.

▼ The ones that got away

As you are sorting through your photographs, try to discard any that are obviously useless; this will help you to establish exactly how many pictures you have and which you want to scrapbook. Although some inferior or damaged photographs can be rescued using photo-manipulation techniques (such as those with 'red eyes'), many cannot be improved and are not worth keeping.

Focus

Not only are this couple's faces out of focus, but they are seated too far away from each other to create any feeling of togetherness.

Lighting

This photograph is dark and murky. The girl's face is hidden and the image is neither strong nor clear enough.

Positioning

Avoid photographs with unintentional humour or unfortunate composition, as they will distract from the theme on your page.

Posed vs spontaneous

Posed photographs, such as school portraits, can feel stiff and do not necessarily look right on a scrapbook page. Try instead to use spontaneous, relaxed snapshots that give a true and more fun feel of the subject's character and personality.

▼ Which is best?

Often you will have several shots of the same event or situation. To thin out your pile of photographs, select one that best captures the moment, then file the rest in an archive of duplicate images and discard inferior photos.

These two photographs were taken at the same time, and would both look good on a scrapbook page. However, the second photograph (below) is probably slightly better, because it imparts a particular impression of warmth and fun.

Avoid clichés

When selecting your best photographs, it is easy to opt for those that portray traditional and familiar poses and situations. But it is often the more unusual photographs that show off your subject's uniqueness. Don't be afraid to use photographs of unsmiling children; people looking at each other instead of into the camera; the blur of movement; or even people's backs – these can all be intriguing when they offer a hint of personality or capture the moment.

Although this photograph shows the subjects walking away, it conveys a sense of the couple's togetherness and the location, such that it may perfectly evoke memories or the particular holiday.

CHAPTER 2

BASIC MATERIALS AND TOOLS

Scrapbook pages can be as simple or as complex as you choose but, whatever your style, you will need some basic equipment and materials to get started. While many of the materials and tools used for scrapbooking are standard for general papercrafting, others, such as adhesives and cardstock, need to be chosen carefully to achieve the best results. This section will guide you through the right products for each aspect of scrapbooking not only to design great-looking pages, but also to ensure that they stand up to being used – and repeatedly turned over – in an album, and that they last for future generations.

CARDSTOCK

Cardstock forms the basic foundation of scrapbook pages. Not only can it be used as a base and support for lighter weight papers and vellums, but also as a main feature of a design. The number of ways in which cardstock can be used makes it an essential purchase and a key part of your supplies.

Treating card

Card can be treated in a number of ways to produce different effects.

Sanding: *Sanding card produces a soft cloudy finish, revealing more of the core with more sanding.*

Crumpling: *Try crumpling card with a white core to break the paper fibres and reveal the contrasting centre.*

Tearing: *Tearing reveals the white centre, offering a contrast that can be further enhanced with other card-breaking techniques.*

◀ **Textures**

Cardstock is also available in a variety of textures. Woven, hammered, linen and ribbed textures can all be used to add visual interest and contribute to the overall style of a page.

▶ **Colours**

Cardstock is available in single colours, which present a uniform colour regardless of whether they are cut, torn or crumpled. Alternatively, for a different look, why not try using cardstock with a white core? Often this will also have two different colour tones on each side. Crumpling and/or cutting will reveal the different layers of colour.

Tip

Scrapbook pages created using just cardstock may be low-cost, but they can look great. You can create mood and feeling on the page through the colours you choose to combine. Take it to the next level by adding stamping, paint or embellishments, and a simple card base can become a stunning canvas for a beautiful design.

PAPER AND VELLUM

Paper and vellum are the wallpaper or background of your scrapbook pages, and are a simple way to add pattern, texture and colour. You will find a wide range available to suit all your themes and pages. It is worth building up a good supply of different patterns and designs, so that you have the perfect paper or vellum ready to hand when you need it.

PAPER

There are almost as many different types of patterned paper as there are wallpaper designs, catering for a wide variety of personal tastes and styles. Matching the mood and style of your pictures to the papers you choose is what makes the difference between a good design and a great one. Patterned papers can also be found pre-embellished with embossing or glitter. These can save time, as they can be used to lift your design quickly and simply out of the ordinary.

Paper types

Co-ordinated paper ranges can make creating beautiful pages a far simpler task than selecting from random designs. Many manufacturers produce collections of patterned papers grouped into colour themes. Different papers from the same range will always work well together in your album. If you are feeling a little more adventurous, try choosing papers from different ranges produced by the same manufacturer. These will tend to be similar in style and theme, but their differences can be emphasised to produce stunning final results.

▲ This scrapbook page uses a muted and soft, patterned paper as a background to complement the photographs and direct the focus on them. An alternative choice of background paper could have resulted in an equally interesting, though quite different, page.

VELLUM

Vellum is a translucent product that adds a soft, cloudy feel to your work. It requires a little care during use to achieve the best results. Like paper, vellum can be found in a host of colours, designs and styles, and is also available embossed or highlighted with glitter. The many varieties of pattern, colour and translucence mean that vellum is a firm favourite with scrapbookers.

▶ Vellum can be plain, patterned, or coloured – and you can also find vellum motifs.

Finding background papers on the internet

If you can't find exactly what you want, or can't get access to a retailer, try downloading patterned papers from the internet and printing them out yourself. There are a huge number of scrapbook-related websites, many of which have digital paper designs available for free. Try www.shabbyprincess.com, www.twopeasinabucket.com, www.scrapbookbytes.com or www.digitalfreebies.com for great free designs.

▲ The addition of a sheet of vellum to this background paper adds a muted, cloudy feel, softening the colours and blurring the pattern.

◀ Why use vellum?

The slightly cloudy quality of vellum makes it perfect for softening brightly coloured card or patterned paper. Experiment by laying a sheet of vellum over different sheets of cardstock and patterned paper to produce muted versions of the original colours. This is also useful for softening strong patterns as well as colours.

Tip

Use vellum to make pockets and envelopes that are perfect for storing memorabilia on the page. The transparent pockets offer a hint of their contents, adding a touch of intrigue to your work.

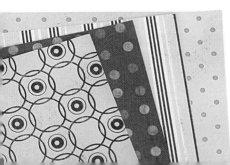

ALBUMS

Albums are available in a whole range of different sizes, formats and colourways – the choice is almost limitless. Deciding what size to work with is very much a matter of personal taste; it is not unusual to have a range of album sizes for a variety of projects at the same time.

An album provides a safe environment for storing completed pages, protecting your work from light and dust. PVC-free page protectors allow your work to be handled safely, protecting the pages from contaminants in the environment and on hands.

Different materials

Albums are available in a wide range of materials, from suede and leather to practical, wipe-clean finishes that can withstand sticky fingers.

Fastenings

Look out for different fastening systems. There is a wide range of different types available, including post-bound, strap-hinge and slide fasteners. Some fastening systems allow more pages to be added easily, without loosening existing contents, while others free all the pages every time they are unlocked.

Folio closure   Ring binder   Post-bound

Which size?

Standard 12x12 inch (30x30cm) scrapbook pages allow space for displaying a number of photographs and comprehensive journaling. Therefore this large format has become hugely popular and there is a wide range of album styles available in different colours, materials, patterns, designs and fastenings.

The 8½x11 inch (21x28cm) page is becoming more popular as it matches paper sizes handled by standard computer printers, providing more options. Albums in this size are available in landscape and portrait formats.

Smaller, 8x8 inch (20x20cm) pages can be faster to design, and require fewer photographs, embellishments and journaling, making them the perfect size for gift albums. A standard 6x4 inch (15x10cm) photograph can be showcased perfectly on this size, in proportion to the rest of the page.

A 6x6 inch (15x15cm) album is economical, as a standard sheet of cardstock can be cut to produce four pages with no waste. Being small, this is the fastest size to complete and these albums make fabulous gifts, or are useful for single themes, such as a special occasion.

Transportable albums

A case-style album is perfect for transporting pages, for example when taking them to classes, or to show friends. This type of album is complete with a handle to make carrying it easy.

ADHESIVES AND GLUES

There is a bewildering range of different adhesives and glues available that are relevant to scrapbooking. It is important to consider in advance what you are looking for, and which product will best suit your particular purpose.

The first and most important thing to look for is an adhesive that is acid-free. Many will also advertise themselves as archival or solvent-free, so take the time to read the packaging carefully. Choosing the right glue will ensure that your designs remain intact and that your photographs are protected and preserved.

Double-sided tabs and tape

Use double-sided adhesive tabs and tapes to attach cardstock, paper and photographs. Thin and permanent, tabs are a fast and clean way to apply adhesive to your projects.

Glue stick

Look for glue sticks labelled 'non-toxic' as these are safe to use on your pages. Glue sticks are available in a variety of sizes.

Repositionable adhesives

Repositionable adhesives allow you to move items around on the page until you are comfortable with the final result. They apply a thin, even layer of glue to one side of an item and are available in a range of sizes.

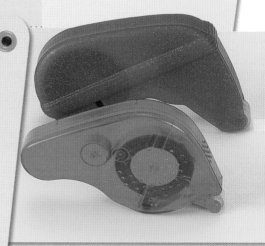

Adhesive spray

Adhesive spray bonds practically any lightweight material instantly, yet also allows work to be lifted and repositioned.

Applying glazes

Simply apply a thin layer of glaze over an embellishment and leave to dry to a crystal-clear glossy shine. Fill frames, conchos and more with glaze to create beautiful page accents.

WHICH GLUE TO USE?

Experiment with scraps of different materials and adhesives to find the best glue for items on your particular scrapbooking project. Use the table below as a general guide.

Glue type	Vellum	Cardstock and paper	Metal	Fabric, ribbon and fibres	Photographs
Glue stick		●			●
Xyron®	●	●	●	●	●
Repositionable dots		●	●	●	●
Glue dots		●	●	●	●
Adhesive tabs				●	
3D tape		●	●		
Double-sided tape		●	●		●
Foam tabs		●	●		●
Glaze			●		
Hi-tack glue		●	●	●	
Vellum tape	●	●			

Modge Podge

Modge Podge is a glue and sealer. It dries clear and works well on decoupage or painted tin projects.

Glazes

Glazes are strong adhesives that can be used to attach metal embellishments and other bulky items to your layouts, and can also be used to add a glossy sheen.

Hi-tack glue

Hi-tack glues form a strong bond ideal for attaching metal, wood or bulky embellishments such as shells to a page. Used sparingly, they are also great for adhering fibres and trimmings.

Adhesive sheets

Double-sided adhesive sheets are a clean and easy way of attaching larger papers and photographs securely.

BASIC TOOLKIT

One of the great aspects of scrapbooking as a craft is that it requires very little in the way of a basic toolkit.

Start with something to cut your card and paper to size – a 12 inch (30cm) trimmer, or a craft knife, metal ruler and a cutting mat will be sufficient. Basic adhesives, both wet and dry, will be necessary to complete a variety of projects and techniques. A simple eyelet toolkit is also worth having. Complete your equipment with a pencil, soft white eraser and a black archival pen, and you are ready to start.

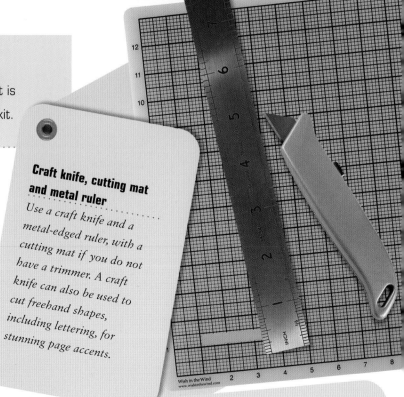

Craft knife, cutting mat and metal ruler

Use a craft knife and a metal-edged ruler, with a cutting mat if you do not have a trimmer. A craft knife can also be used to cut freehand shapes, including lettering, for stunning page accents.

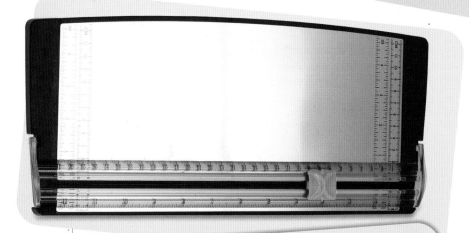

12 inch (30cm) trimmer

The standard 12x12 inch (30x30cm) format scrapbook cardstock and paper can be trimmed to size quickly using a 12 inch (30cm) trimmer. Blade types and cutting systems vary, and some trimmers offer scoring and fancy blades for various effects.

Archival pens

Add journaling to your scrapbook pages with an archival pen, which is formulated to be light-fast and photo-safe. Handwritten journaling with an archival pen adds more than just the story – it offers a glimpse of your personality.

Journal Pen
ACID FREE • PERMANENT • FADE RESISTANT

Acid-Testing Pen

Dark Paper Pen

Scissors

Scissors are the mainstay of any craft kit. As well as for standard cutting, scissors can also be used to score and curl paper for interesting effects.

Pencil and eraser

A standard pencil is one of the most useful tools in your kit. Use it for marking and measuring, creating straight lines for journaling and titles, and a great deal more. A soft white eraser removes pencil marks, and can also be used to remove excess chalk from your designs.

Camera

A camera is the essential item for any scrapbooker as it produces the key element of your pages – your photographs. Modern cameras take much of the guesswork out of photography, with pre-set programs that sort out the technicalities for you.

Eyelet toolkit

An eyelet toolkit, consisting of a hammer, punch, setter and mat, will form a staple of your toolkit. There are also eyelet tools that can punch and set without a hammer, which reduces the number of items in your toolbox.

EMBELLISHMENTS

Embellishments are the finishing touches for your scrapbook pages. They are like the accessories you wear with your clothes and can really make a difference to the overall look of your work. Like fashion accessories, embellishments are available in a huge range and include charms, buttons, ribbons, buckles, beads, fibres, pressed flowers, die cuts and more.

BEADS *All sorts of beads can be stuck straight on pages as decoration or threaded on decorative cotton, rings or wire to make charms. Tiny beads can be used for edging or in corner designs. Little patches of bead work – or beading – can be pinned to pages.*

BELLS *Tiny bells can be attached to your pages with ribbon. They are ideal for weddings, baby themes or festive pages.*

BRADS *Brads are wire clips with decorative tops. They slip through eyelets or small holes and open out flat at the back. They make great decorations and are useful for attaching items.*

BUTTONS *There is a wide choice of buttons available, both plain and decorative. Flat buttons can be used with wire, wool, ribbon or twine. They can be glued in place or hung as charms. Try using different sizes of the same type or design.*

CHARMS *All sorts of charms can be purchased from craft suppliers or department stores. Thread them on rings, slip them over paperclips, pin them with safety pins or attach with wire or ribbon. Make your own charms with beads, buttons or inexpensive jewellery.*

CLIPS, CLASPS AND FASTENERS *Paper clips, hair clips or grips, clasps for jewellery or clothes and clothes fasteners are all great embellishments. Glue them in place and use them to attach notes or layers of paper and card.*

CRAFT MIRRORS *Tiny mirrors can be used to trim pages or on picture frames. They can be stuck on discs and hung as charms.*

CRAFT TWINE *There is a vast choice of craft twine, in all sorts of textures and colours. Use it to hang embellishments, lay it across pages, or tuck labels and pictures under it.*

CROSS STITCH MOTIFS *Tiny patches of cross stitch work (bought or home-made) can be used to reflect many themes – seasonal, baby, wedding or birthday dates.*

CRYSTALS *Little crystals can be glued to pages, or ring attachments (for hanging), or placed in mini acetate bags and glued or hung.*

CUT-OUTS *Cut-outs come in all shapes, colours, finishes and sizes from craft suppliers. Make your own using a cut-out punch.*

DECORATIVE SCISSORS *Scissors with blades that cut decorative shapes, these can be used for papers or fabrics.*

DIE CUTS *Intricate shapes can be purchased to complement every theme. Die cutting kits are also available to cut out your own shapes.*

EMBOSSING *Powders, pads with pens and embossing tools can all be used on card or paper to create plaques, frames or labels. Some powders are heated so they melt in place.*

ENVELOPES AND FOLDERS *Buy or make mini envelopes, or make mini folders from card or paper. Use them to hold greetings and messages.*

EYELETS *Placed through holes made with a punch and flattened with a special tool, eyelets can be decorative, and used for threading wire, twine or ribbon to attach items to pages. Several items can be attached in the same eyelet.*

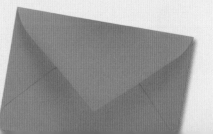

FABRICS Swatches and strips of fabrics can be used as backgrounds, trimmings or ties. Snip pieces from hidden areas inside wedding garments or favourite items to complement photographs.

FANTASY FILM SHAPES Fantasy film is a liquid that sets to resemble glass over dipped wire loops. Good for petal shapes and charms.

FEATHERS Fun or sophisticated, feathers are available in all sorts of colours. Hang them on charms or tuck them under layers of card.

FIBRES Spiderweb is one of a number of fine fibres that can be pulled into a soft, mist-like swatch. Metallic, synthetic, wool, cotton and textured fibres can be tied or glued to pages. Take fibres from favourite garments, or raid your needlework kit.

FOAMIES Craft foam comes in sheets or cut-outs, in lots of colours, ready to glue or with self-adhesive backing. There are lots of different finishes. Use foam for a three-dimensional effect.

FRAMES Buy or make card mounts to frame pictures or decorations. Fine wood frames are useful – look out for doll's house frames to pick out embellishments. Make frames from fabric, folded paper or acetate and tissue. Add decorative items, ties and tags.

GEMS Imitation gems can be attached individually or as part of a design. They can be placed on a page or used on little medals to make charms. Some are self-adhesive, others have to be glued in place.

GILDING Use powders, paint or inexpensive metal-leaf papers to gild areas of pages. Confectionery wrappers (especially from the more expensive chocolates) make great gilding patches – smooth them under a piece of cotton fabric using a cool iron, then stick them on your page.

GLITTER Sprinkle glitter over patches of glue; or used glitter glue pens to write or draw designs.

HOLOGRAPHIC FOILS In sheets or cut-outs these add a three-dimensional feel to pages. Use them as background, for frames, or under acetate titles or labels.

INKS Use inks for stamping, painting or edging. They come in a variety of colours and applications. Look out for metallic inks.

LEATHER THONGING Leathercraft supplies can be used for decorating scrapbook pages. Strips of thonging can be used to tie tags in place, or attached at each end as a tuck-under strip. Leather offcuts or tags can be embossed or punched with decorative finishes.

MINI CLOTHES PEGS In wood or plastic, these can be stuck onto a page and then tags or items can be pegged in them.

PLAQUES Make little plaques from shrink plastic, air-dry clay, card, or used metal or fine wood shapes. Add tiny frames or other features. Print out messages in small type and glue to a plaque if you don't want to write or paint by hand.

POM-POMS Glue them straight on a page, or hang them from ribbons. Great for bookmark ends. Fluffy pom-poms come in all sorts of colours, and in metallic or glitter finish.

PRESSED FLOWERS Fresh flowers can be pressed, or use dried flowers, or cut-out flowers from fine papers. Use bought stamens, beans and sparkles for centres.

PUNCHES Punches can be used to cut out decorative edges, shapes and letters from paper or card.

RECORDING BUTTONS These are available ready to record your own memorable sounds – you can capture your child's first laugh or words and preserve them on your pages.

Tip

You do not need to use a lot of items to decorate your pages; one or two carefully chosen elements can be all that are needed to add something special to your design. Look for embellishments that match the style, colour or overall feel of your photographs.

RIBBON ROSES *Tiny roses in all sorts of colours – glue them onto pages, on frames, or on strips of ribbon or card.*

RIBBONS *Use ribbon for edging, linking photographs, attaching embellishments and decorating pages. Tie bows, loops or drape it in swirls, gluing them in place at intervals. Lay ribbon under mounts or over pictures.*

RUB-ONS *Individual characters or numerals, shapes and decorations can be bought as rub-ons, ready to be positioned and rubbed off the film straight on to the page, or over photographs. Position them carefully, making sure the spelling is right when rubbing on a title.*

SEAGRASS *A popular alternative to twine, use seagrass to wrap around sections of card or page, to attach items or as a trimming.*

SELF-ADHESIVE FELT *In sheets ready to cut or as cut-outs, this can be used as a background or mount for frames, or to make decorative leaves or flowers.*

SEQUINS *Sticky or for gluing in place, these can be used in a pattern, randomly to brighten a page, or individually. Add them to charms, thread them on fine metal thread, or use them in flower centres.*

SHRINK PLASTIC *Special heat-shrink kits can be used to shrink printed photographs, messages or pieces of artwork to miniature form. Great for making little tags or charms.*

SPARKLES *Glittery bits and pieces to buy and use for decorating pages. Stick them on or attach them under squares of acetate, so they move about.*

SQUEAKERS *Tiny squeakers sold for toys or cards can be fun on scrapbook pages. Especially good for baby features.*

STAMPS *Stamping is a classic technique for scrapbooking. Wooden or plastic stamps are available in every type of design. Make your own stamps using ready-made kits or by using a foam die cut out.*

STENCILS *Craft suppliers sell miniature stencils that can be used repeatedly. Characters, numerals, and decorative shapes or designs are available. Stencil with pencil, paint, ink or glue and glitter. Add messages or designs to pages, frames, tags or acetate overlays.*

STICKERS *Every craft supplier offers lots of stickers. Select them carefully, to suit the design and theme. Position them on strap lines, frames or mounts.*

TAGS *Tags can be used in many different shapes and materials. They are ideal for adding messages. Let them hang on ribbon, twine or fabric strips, or use small loops of card, leather or folded paper to place them firmly on the page.*

TRANSFERS *Just like rub-ons, there are all sorts of transfers available for adding decorative finishes to backgrounds, photo corners, frames and labels. Create and print out your own transfers using computer printer kits.*

WIRE *As well as beading wire, cake decorating wire and craft wire, look for fine garden and floristry wire. Twist wire into shapes for decorating pages, especially over mounting cards. Glue fine paper over wire shapes for an interesting effect. Use wire to attach embellishments.*

WOOD SHAPES *Tiny wood shapes can be used for plaques or as a base for gems and crystals. They are ideal for mounting fragments of items or clothing.*

Bought embellishments or found objects?

There is a wide range of exciting and stylish embellishments available to be bought and it is often easy to find the exact item that a page seems to need. Remember, however, that embellishments do not have to cost a fortune. You can use found objects or everyday items to create stunning designs for no money at all. Shells and sand, dried leaves, pressed flowers, scraps of fabric and old jewellery can all be used to co-ordinate with the theme of your page. With a little imagination, clever trinkets can be made and applied to every type of page.

Bought items

Found objects

CHAPTER 3

MAKING THE MOST OF YOUR PHOTOS

One of the key purposes of scrapbooking your photographs is to show them off to their best possible advantage. Choosing the right colours to complement your pictures is important to bring out the best in them. Colour theory is not complex and this chapter will demonstrate some of the key considerations when deciding which colours to use.

Sometimes less is more – taking away some of your photograph by cropping it can actually make the image much more meaningful. Mounting photos is another way to make the most of them, drawing attention to key composition features and focusing on the important themes for pages.

USING COLOUR WITH PHOTOS

Having the confidence to match colours with your photographs can make a huge difference to the impact of your creative work. Colour theory is one of the 'elements of art' that includes line, colour, shape, form, space and texture. This set of principles can be used to create harmonious colour combinations that will lift your work out of the ordinary.

THE COLOUR WHEEL

Colour relationships can be explored using a colour wheel, which is created by wrapping the spectrum around to connect the ends together in a circle. Use of colour theory and the colour wheel can help you select colours that work well together, both with your photographs and each other.

Matching colours

Select one of the colours from within your chosen photograph and then match it with different combinations from the colour wheel to find the most visually pleasing set of colours for complementary use on the page. If you can't find a scheme that works well with your photographs, try changing them to black and white. Black-and-white pictures are colour-neutral and can be successfully combined with any other colour scheme.

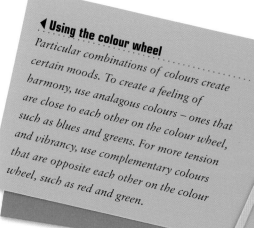

◀ **Using the colour wheel**
Particular combinations of colours create certain moods. To create a feeling of harmony, use analagous colours – ones that are close to each other on the colour wheel, such as blues and greens. For more tension and vibrancy, use complementary colours that are opposite each other on the colour wheel, such as red and green.

CHOOSING COLOUR SCHEMES

▼ Monochrome

Monochrome schemes use variations in light and dark, and saturation of a single colour. They tend to be clean and elegant – tones of one colour are easy on the eye and can be soothing.

▲ Complementary

Complementary colours are directly opposite each other on the colour wheel. These produce high-contrast designs, with each colour making the other appear brighter, and more vivid, than it is alone. Use complementary colours for dynamic, energetic pages that really "pop".

▼ Triadic

Triadic colour schemes are created from three equally spaced colours on the wheel. These colours tend to have a strong visual contrast while maintaining a feeling of harmony. The overall effect of triadic schemes is one of balance and harmony.

The creativity of colour

Colour attracts the viewer: it opens up the whole design and brings an additional dimension to the appearance of a layout. By changing the density of the colour you are using, you can make it look as if another colour is being used – and, of course, it creates contrast within the overall composition.

▶ Introducing borders in complementary colours is a great way of adding visual variety.

▶ There is a pleasing contrast between the white of the text and the deep blue of the sky, making the title easy to read. The positioning of the title is also an effective use of space.

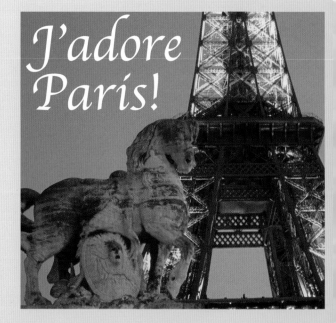

▶ Selecting colours

Some colours appear to advance, while others seem to recede. If you want to make something seem to come towards the viewer, warm colours, such as reds and oranges, are the best ones to choose. Cooler colours, such as blues and greens, seem to recede, especially when set next to a red.

▼ Colour and legibility

The colour of your type will affect its legibility and impact. When using different colours on a white background, the colour needs to be strong and advance, rather than recede. If you use a coloured background and coloured type, the two colours must work together or the type will not be legibile.

advance   **advance**

recede   **recede**

A clash of background and type colour makes type illegible.

Contrasting background and type works well even though the background is patterned.

Advancing colour type on a monotone background works well.

HOW TO TAKE BETTER PHOTOS

It can be extremely disappointing to send a roll of film to be developed and have a series of less-than-perfect pictures come back, especially if this means some very important events have not been captured as you would have wished. To reduce the chances of this happening, you can easily learn a few techniques that will help you to begin to take better photos.

PHOTOGRAPHING PEOPLE

A good photograph of a person should capture something of their essence – showing their personality, emotions and age in one brief moment. A good portrait can be the key that holds your whole scrapbook page together, so it is worth learning how to make them as good as possible.

Go digital!

If you can, take pictures with a digital camera. Digital photography provides instant feedback as you work and offers the opportunity to retake the shot immediately. Digital pictures are also free, so you can afford to take more shots of the same subject, increasing the chances of getting that great picture. About 1 in 20 shots that you take will be really good, and only 1 or 2 in 100 will be great, so it stands to reason that the more pictures you take, the better the chances of taking a really great photo.

▶ Zooming in close

To capture your subject's personality, try zooming in really close, filling your viewfinder with their face to force attention onto your subject, and remove the chance of a distracting background. Don't be afraid to chop off the top of your subject's head, as in this photograph – it can make the picture more powerful and striking.

Tip

Interesting lighting, and capturing a positive, or fascinating, side to your subject's personality, are features to look for when you zoom close in. Filling the frame with character is important: shooting the telltale expression, and physical detail, such as perfect or slightly flawed skin, will not detract from the overall image.

Different angles

Try photographing portraits from a variety of different angles, rather than just straight on.

This photograph, taken from a lower vantage point looking up at the subjects, captures a sense of fun and liveliness and creates an eye-catching portrait.

This photograph is taken from a high vantage point and works well by capturing all the key elements of the event in a single shot.

▶ Portrait or landscape?

Choosing between taking a portrait or a landscape shot is a crucial point. When photographing one person, a vertical composition is usually best because people are much taller than they are wide (this is why the term 'portrait' is used). When photographing groups, or when you want to show more of the background, a horizontal or landscape format is more suitable. However, it also depends on which elements you wish to emphasise.

The portrait format (left) focuses attention on the closeness of the father and daughter, whereas the landscape format (right) is better for capturing the movement of the sparklers.

This shot works because of the intimate, tiny details – the neat nail polish, the elegantly crossed legs, and the one-shoe-on, one-shoe off pose – which all suggest both relaxation and glamour.

◀ Be unconventional

Experiment with portraits that do not include a face; focus on hands, feet or the curve of a shoulder for a picture that evokes emotion and tells more of a story.

This portrait, focusing on the subject's eye, increases the sense of the subject's personality, as well as providing a very personal, up-close portrait.

▶ Using backgrounds

An effective background to the subject of your photograph can make all the difference between an ordinary photo and a compelling one. Background elements, such as poles sticking out of the top of a subject's head, can ruin your photograph, whereas a controlled background can complement and focus it. If you are taking a simple portrait, consider using a sheet of coloured paper or cardboard as a background.

In the first photograph (left) the patterned background contrasts sharply with the man's shirt, leaving the viewer eye confused and bewildered. Moving the subject to a plain white background (right) solves the problem and refocuses the attention.

Tip

Remember that with digital photography, you can use photo-manipulation programs to modify the background later.

▶ Action shots

Taking action shots can be a challenging way to capture movement and excitement. Start by setting your camera to 'sports' mode if it has one. This will allow you to take more shots in a short space of time. The next thing to do is keep shooting. Things are changing continually with action shots, so you need to think and act faster. Move with your subject to keep them in your viewfinder and in focus. Alternatively, allow your subject to move through the shot for a blurred, dynamic photograph that captures a feeling of speed.

Although there is some blurring in this photograph, it captures the feeling of movement and fun of the subject.

This photograph has captured the movement of the subject so well that the young boy appears to be suspended in mid-air. The expression of delight on his face adds to the life and fun of the photograph.

Framing

Once you have tried out some of these tips, experiment by framing your subject in unusual ways. Try off-setting the subject to one side of your shot to create an interesting, dynamic image where the space in the shot is as important as the subject. Take inspiration from pictures that you particularly like, and try to recreate these for yourself – the process will help you to learn more about your camera and composition.

CROPPING PHOTOGRAPHS

The term 'cropping' means to remove part of an image so as to emphasise the focus. Cropping draws attention to the main subject of the photograph, removing any distracting elements in the shot. It can also be used to draw the focal point back to the centre of a poorly composed shot. Cropping can be done while framing a subject in the camera viewfinder or later by physically removing some of a photograph, for example by cutting it off or masking it out.

Making a viewing frame

It can often be difficult to decide whether a photo would be improved by cropping. When this is the case, try making two 'L' shapes from plain card and place these at diagonally opposite corners of the picture. Move the 'L' shapes across the picture, increasing and decreasing the size of the aperture – or space – over the photo until you find the most visually pleasing area. Mark the inside four corners of the photograph with a wax pencil and remove the 'L' shapes. Trim the picture to the four marks to finish cropping.

Placing focus

A simple image can be cropped in a number of different ways. It is up to you to decide which elements of a photograph form the main focus. By closing in on a particular detail or area you can easily add drama and interest.

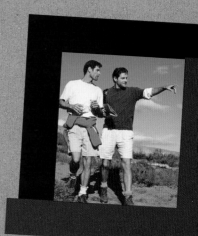

Cropping with a craft knife

Place a metal ruler over the photograph, aligning it with the grid on the cutting mat underneath. Use a craft knife to cut against the edge of the ruler.

Different-shaped crops

You can crop your photographs in different shapes. If you can find a suitable template to cut around, you can shape your photos accordingly, from circles and hearts to stars and hexagons. Here, a handy household cup has been used to carefully crop this photograph in a circle shape.

Tip

If you are uncertain whether or not to crop a picture, opt to create a frame or border that will perform the same task. Place the intact photograph under the frame, effectively cropping the unwanted sections while preserving the whole picture. Overlapping and layering items can be a good way of masking or cropping unwanted areas of an image.

Make copies

Always make copies of precious pictures before cropping them. This is particularly important with heritage pictures, where the distracting background elements that may not bring out the best in your page design can contain important historical information. Only ever crop the copy in these circumstances and store the original in a safe environment. That superfluous detail on one page may be the perfect choice of complementary image for a different theme on another project.

MOUNTING PHOTOGRAPHS

Mounting (also known as matting) is a quick and simple way to draw attention to a photograph on your scrapbook page. A photo mount acts in much the same way as a frame around a picture – it emphasises the importance of the picture and finishes it off.

SIZE AND COLOUR

A mount is simply a piece of card cut slightly larger than the length and width of the photograph that sits on it. The size of a mount can vary according to requirements and personal preference: leave ¼ inch (5mm), ½ inch (1cm) or ¾ inch (2cm) of exposed border – there are no rules.

You could choose to use basic black or white card as a mount for a strong clean look, or you could highlight a colour from the photograph with a complementary coloured mount. If you are feeling more adventurous, try using patterned paper to create a decorative mount.

Tip

Experiment with different materials as mounts, including, for example, metal sheets, fabric or mulberry paper. Mounting a photo can give it a visual 'lift' on the page and emphasise it as a focal point of your design.

Creating a mount

▶ Make more of a photograph as the focal point of your scrapbook page by mounting it onto co-ordinating card. Use a trimmer and dry adhesive to achieve the best results.

◀ Apply adhesive to the reverse of your photograph and place it at the top corner of a sheet of card leaving an even border along the top edge and one side.

▶ Trim the remaining side and bottom edges to the same width as the top border, using a trimmer to produce a neatly mounted photograph.

Using mounts on your pages

A formal photograph usually works best with a formal style of photo mount. Here, the photograph has been triple mounted using rich colours and evenly sized borders to complement the formal pose of the subject.

Bring visual interest to photo mounts by, quite literally, adding a twist. One of the layers of this double mount has been laid at an angle, for an unusual take on the standard photo treatment.

Types of mount

There are many different types and styles of mount. Experiment with different widths and note the effect that the mount has on the impact of your pictures. Add layers of co-ordinating or contrasting colours, using double and triple mounts with photographs to draw your design together. A double mount consists of a frame of two colours of card layered together. Varying the width of each mount draws the eye and adds visual interest. Take it up a level by triple mounting your key, focal-point photograph. Triple mounting a picture will quickly and simply establish it as the important image in your design.

Single mount

A single mount is one layer of card, paper or other material used as a base to bring out the best in your photograph.

Double mount

The standard double mount consists of two layers of card that work well with the photograph. A single mount is cut and then this is attached to a second layer, allowing a narrow border around the first.

Reverse double mount

Reverse the standard double mount by cutting a narrow single mount to start. The second layer is cut with a wide border to reveal more of the co-ordinating cardstock.

Triple mount

Place a double-mounted photograph onto a third layer of card and cut a further border. Try alternating card colours for a sophisticated look, or use three different layers for a fun and fresh effect.

DIGITAL PHOTO MANIPULATION

Almost everyone has a selection of less-than-perfect photographs that need a little help to improve them. Digital photo manipulation can help to fix some of the problems in unsuccessful pictures so that they can take pride of place in your albums.

To take full advantage of the opportunities that digital photo manipulation offers, your pictures first need to be in a digital format – either taken with a digital camera or scanned into your computer. Use photo-manipulation software (such as Photoshop) to open a copy of your image, and then experiment with some of the tools available for you to use. Always work on a copy to be sure that the original remains safe and available for future use.

The basics

Before moving on to digital work, you can start with 'low-tech' photo manipulation by using a red-eye removal pen. This provides an instant fix for the reflection of a flash in the eyes of your subjects. Apply a series of small dots over the area of red-eye to build up the coverage until the reflection disappears. The red-eye pen will only work on photos developed in a laboratory – pictures printed on a home inkjet printer cannot be repaired in this way.

Cropping and resizing

Use the cropping tool to trim away distracting backgrounds, centre your subject or zoom in on one particular section. Cropping digitally means that you will save ink when printing out your photographs as only the section you want will actually be printed. Resizing a photograph can be achieved very simply using photo-manipulation software. At the click of a button you can enlarge a snapshot into a high-impact image.

The original photograph (far left) has been cropped and resized (left) to bring the focus in more clearly on the subject and exclude much of the unnecessary background.

▼ Changing the colour

One of the most enjoyable aspects of digital enhancement is being able to change the colour of any element in the picture. If you photographed someone wearing a red top that now looks too bright, you can change it to green or pink – or any colour you like. Just select the area you want to change, then choose the colour to replace it. Be careful, however, to select all of the item, and exclude all areas of any other object of similar colour.

▲ Converting to black and white

You can also remove colour altogether by converting a photograph to black and white. Look for an option to change to greyscale and, with a single click, your picture will be transformed. Some photographs can be very difficult to work with due to the colour combinations within them. Switching to black and white can solve this problem.

Cloning

The 'clone' tool allows you to duplicate one section of your photograph to another position on your image. This is a great tool for removing scratches, covering blemishes and filling in damaged sections of the photograph. You will often find that you will have the option to alter the size of the clone brush, opt for a smaller brush for delicate or tricky sections, and increase the brush size for larger areas.

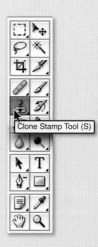

Clone Stamp Tool (S)

In the first image (above left), the object in the background merges with the woman's head in a distracting and unintentionally humorous way. The cloning tool can be used to copy the colour of the background and then paint over the object to remove it.

CHAPTER 4

DESIGNING SCRAPBOOK PAGES

Designing a scrapbook page can be a challenge but it is also immensely rewarding. This chapter will lead you through the basic design principles that can make the difference between good pages and great ones.

The guidelines in this section will help you to establish a focal point, incorporate multiple photographs and use the principles of good composition effectively. You will also see how using preparatory sketches as an aid to design can help to create pages quickly and effectively. Getting it right by drawing up 'roughs' saves time and avoids tedious mistakes; it also helps to ensure you remember to include all the important items you wanted to display. These are not rules to be followed strictly, but helpful advice that will help you to produce scrapbooks that you can feel proud of.

ELEMENTS OF A PAGE

A scrapbook page is made up of a number of different elements. When you design pages, think about how the different elements will work together. Will they clash or will they complement each other?

2 Embellishments

Embellishments add the finishing touches to your page. Choosing the right embellishment to match the colour, style and theme is a knack that you will develop with experience.
(see Embellishments, pages 26-29)

1 Frames and borders

Both photographs and the whole page can benefit from a frame or border to centre and focus attention.
(see Borders, page 56)

3 Photographs

Photographs are the main focus of your pages. Once you have selected the photos, there are a number of ways of using and displaying them.
(see Using Many Photos, pages 64–73)

5 Journaling

Journaling can range from just a few basic facts to long passages filled with your thoughts and memories. Whether hidden, using hinges and envelopes, or on full display, journaling is an important feature.
(see The Art of Journaling, pages 82–93)

where have the years gone?

4 Title

The title sets the tone of your page. The style and position is every bit as important as the words themselves in reinforcing the theme.
(see Arranging Words, page 58 and Styles of Lettering, page 62)

EXPLORING COMPOSITION

You do not need the knowledge and skills of a graphic designer to create well-composed scrapbook pages. By building on a few simple design techniques, you can create layouts that will be visually pleasing and well-balanced.

POSITIONING TITLES

Every scrapbook page involves arranging two key elements: photographs and words. Let's start with words: experiment with positioning a single line to represent a heading; this could be for your title page. Move the line around inside the page shape to establish where it presents the most visually dynamic position within the space. As you do this you'll find that you are more naturally attracted to some positions than others. This discovery is the first in the natural creative process.

Tip

Remember, in the early stages of planning a scrapbook page it's easier to work on smaller, scaled-down versions of the actual design. You can sketch many of these on a single sheet of paper and compare them easily with each other.

CHANGING THE TITLE PROPORTIONS

The next step is to expand and contract the title proportions to see how much of the scrapbook page you want it to occupy. Pay attention to the space left when the title is in position and at the right size. Balance the space with the weight – size and density – of the text, leaving more white space at the top, bottom and side if the title looks 'weighty' or too heavy.

TITLE

Try making the title the dominant element on the page.

Also experiment with the title used in a more subtle way.

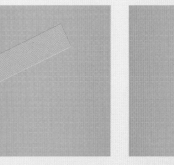

INTRODUCING MORE TEXT

There are many occasions when you will want to incorporate more than one line or title into your page. The additional lines may not be a title, but a caption that tells more about a picture, or a little piece of journaling – some background information, not specifically related to a picture.

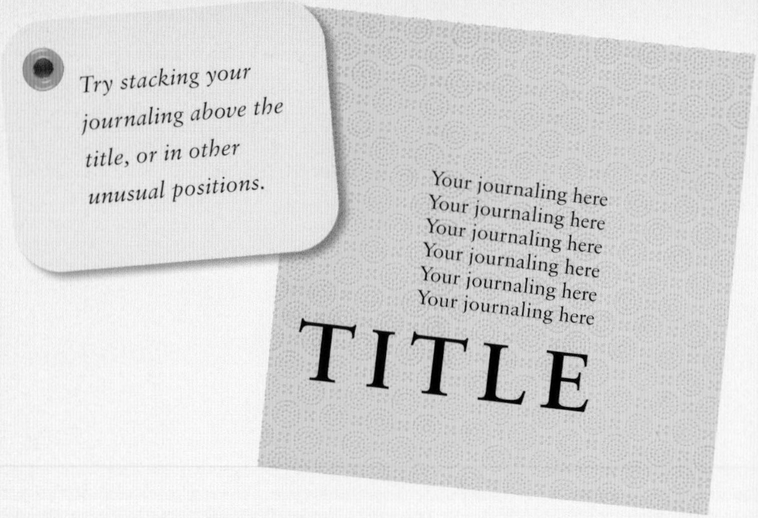

Try stacking your journaling above the title, or in other unusual positions.

Your journaling here
Your journaling here
Your journaling here
Your journaling here
Your journaling here
Your journaling here

TITLE

TITLE

Your journaling here
Your journaling here
Your journaling here
Your journaling here

Your journaling
here Your
journaling here
Your journaling

TITLE

here Your
journaling here
Your journaling
here Your
journaling here
Your journaling
here Your
journaling here
Your journaling

here Your
journaling here
Your journaling
here Your
journaling here
Your journaling
here Your
journaling here
Your journaling
here Your
journaling here
Your journaling
hereYour journaling
here Your
journaling here

Experiment with different ways of having the title breaking into your journaling.

PLACING PHOTOS AND MEMORABILIA

Introduce photographs and memorabilia before finalising the precise design or look of your headings and captions. Before sticking down any item, experiment with its position and its relationship to the words, title or other items.

Experiment with different shapes by cutting them out of coloured cartridge paper.

Decide which shape and position gives the most successful effect.

Keep shapes roughly to the same scale as each other.

ALLOCATING SPACE

How much space should your photos occupy? Naturally, the size of the photographs will be affected by the other elements or components you want to include in the overall design. At this stage, your first aim is to experiment creatively.

Move the shapes around the design area to find a pleasing composition.

Experiment with alternative design arrangements.

BRINGING WORDS AND PICTURES TOGETHER

You are now aware of the possibilities of manipulating lines that represent titles and text, and shapes that represent photographs and memorabilia; and the space these separate features can occupy. Next, experiment with ways of combining these elements on the page.

The line that represents your heading can be flexible in size, length and weight.

TITLE

The picture shape can be made bigger or smaller.

Have a look at these layouts: some alternative combinations should occur to you.

INTRODUCING EXTRA TEXT

Now the fun begins. Expand the design by bringing in more text and the story you are telling. This additional text is journaling in scrapbooking terminology.

TITLE

Your journaling here Your journaling here Your journaling

You may want to organise the lines of text into columns, such as you would see in a newspaper or magazine.

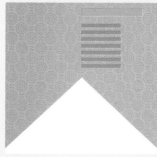

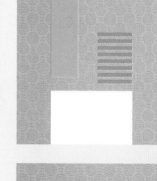

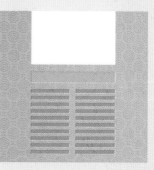

FOCAL POINT

The focal point of a design is the centre of interest, the place your eyes are drawn to. On a well-designed page, this will be the key photograph that you want to highlight. The focal point can be established by using a number of different tricks, including manipulating the colour, size and placement.

▼ Size

Make a photo large and you will almost definitely make it the focus of the page. A large picture will dominate the design and attract attention. Use this technique when working with multiple pictures, and make one shot larger than the others to create a focal point.

▲ Rule of thirds

Another design principle that can help to establish a focal point is the 'rule of thirds'. Imagine your page divided down into three equal columns and across into three sections to make nine equal squares. Place your photograph on one of the intersecting lines. These places on the page are the most prominent and naturally draw the eye. Placing your main picture on one of these intersections adds more visual weight to it. For larger pictures, try positioning a key element of your photograph, such as a person's eyes or face, over the intersection to achieve the same effect.

COLOUR THEORY

Colour theory can help with the choice of colour combinations but it can sometimes be tricky to establish the amount of each colour to use.

LAUGHTER SILLY HAPPINE

COUSINS ARE COOL

Grandparents create
a chain of love
linking the past
with the future.
The chain may lengthen
but it will never break

LOVE

Quart, pint, ounce

Using three colours, or colour tones, in different proportions can have a significant impact upon the finished result – using a large amount of one main colour, a 'quart' – this would usually be the main background colour and will be dominant. Use a 'pint' of a second colour – approximately a third as much as the main colour – for elements such as photo mounts. Finally, an 'ounce' of a third colour will add a spark of drama and excitement. Try creating titles, tags and other embellishments from your ounce of colour.

Visual triangle

You can guide the eye around your design, taking the viewer to each element in turn, through use of another theory called 'the visual triangle'. Arranging elements on your page in a triangular shape helps the eye to move between them and rest on each in turn. A triangle is a restful way to guide the viewer around the page so that they take in a lot of information. The visual triangle can be emphasised by placing repeating elements at each apex.

BORDERS

Borders are an established way to embellish your scrapbook pages, creating the theme and adding a decorative accent to your work. Borders can be as simple or complex as you choose, to fit with your personal style of scrapbooking.

A simple border can be placed on any or all of the four sides of a layout. Experiment with placing borders on each side to see exactly how it affects the overall balance of the page.

Advantages of a border

A border, whether it has four sides, two or just one, helps to frame and define a photograph or scrapbook page. It places the picture or pictures and guides the eye towards the chosen centre of focus. In these examples, the page looks bare and undefined without a border. The border helps to give it a lift and purpose.

Side borders

A side border affects how your eye moves over the page – you can use this to guide the eye to particular parts of your design.

The above page looks loose, almost as if the images are going to fall off the page. With the border in place (left), the page has structure and looks complete.

Tip

Remember that, although a border can add a much-needed finishing touch, it needs to complement and work with the existing elements of the page. Think about the colours and styles used and choose a-border that will bring out the best in them.

Textured borders

Be bold with your choice of materials for borders. Cardstock and patterned paper may form the basis of your design but they are not the only materials available. Fabric, metal sheet, mesh, ribbons, fibres and much more can all be used to make visually interesting borders. Use punches, tags, charms, silk flowers and other decorative items to create borders that add that 'something special' to your work and lift it out of the ordinary.

Types of border

You can use a variety of styles of borders, each offsetting your page in a different way.

Wide border

Narrow border

Deckle-edge border

Shaped border: circle

Shaped border: star

Side border: bottom

Side border: top

Side border: left

Side border: right

ARRANGING WORDS

The best placement of all elements is essential for creating balance and harmony in your designs. The use of titles and text on your scrapbook pages sets the tone and theme, and gives the viewer an indication of the story behind the photographs. The style and words should complement one another, reinforcing the theme of the design, and matching the mood of your photographs and embellishments.

POSITIONING TITLES

There are various ways of positioning a title on a page: it can be ranged left (in other words, with each line aligned to the left), ranged right or centred. You can also change the direction of type from horizontal to vertical, set type at an angle, or even break away from the convention of setting it in a straight line.

Try using the line of a semicircle or curve to position the title.

Centre the title and place it just above the midline to create an even appearance.

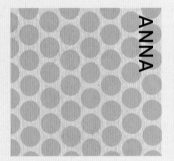

Breaking away from the traditional direction of text can increase tension.

When the title is placed at the bottom of the page it holds attention and looks strong.

The title can be placed near the top of the page, but other elements must balance the design.

Positioning type near the edge of the page implies movement and increases tension.

A different angle creates visual contrast, but background pattern and layout must be used carefully.

For a strong design statement, try enlarging the type to cover the full width of the page.

Reducing the size of type can be effective if it is complemented by the other features.

MAKING THE WORDS LEGIBLE

The spacing and legibility of your words can have a huge effect on the look and feel of your page. This is especially important when using computer-generated text but can also apply to handwriting. Learning how to use leading, tracking and kerning will give your pages a truly professional feel.

▶ Leading

The amount of leading (spacing between lines of text) you use depends on how the letters fit with each other. There is no right or wrong amount – you simply have to decide on the effect you want to create. You may have to achieve visually interesting lines at the expense of legibility.

▶ Tracking

The tracking function on computers adjusts the amount of space to the right-hand side of characters in a highlighted range. You have to use your own judgement about what looks best.

▶ Kerning

The kerning function adjusts the amount of space between two letters. It can be especially important when designing headings or short phrases.

▶ Typeface weight

Changing the weight of a typeface provides many different options. Here, Helvetica is presented in light, medium and bold. Which one you choose will depend upon the effect you are aiming for.

Changing weight gives options

Changing weight gives options

Changing weight gives options

The best designers use their eyes and trust their judgement.

The best designers use their eyes and trust their judgement.

Tracking at -10

Tracking at 10

Tracking at 30

Tracking at 50

Kerning is a useful tool for controlling the space between c h a r a c t e r s.

Tip

Take inspiration from adverts, books and magazines, and product packaging for your titles. These often use great colours, clear fonts and unusual text placement to catch the eye, and these techniques can work on your scrapbook pages. If you find something you really like, sketch it, photograph it or tear it out and keep it in an idea book for inspiration in the future.

DESIGNING WITH WORDS

The style in which you set journaling passages will depend on the other elements of the page – the photographs, embellishments and format. It is relatively easy to set the type in irregular shapes, centre it or range it from different directions. The format of the page will also influence how you set the type: landscape formats can accommodate wider measures (or widths) of text, while portrait formats need shorter measures.

▼ Symmetry

Symmetrical arrangements can successfully accommodate justified settings as well as centring each line.

▼ Aligning text

Asymmetrical compositions can rag the copy left or right.

▼ Mixing styles

Asymmetrical compositions can rag the copy left or right. Try to avoid mixing two styles of setting. Although it can occasionally look quite funky, it often just looks messy and cluttered.

Force justified

Justified type aligns on both the left and the right. However, this style can look visually poor if the measure or lines are too short, as the space between words can be excessive.

Rag left

Ragged-left settings with an off-centred composition give an asymmetrical arrangement. This style tends to be more dynamic than a symmetrical style of setting.

Stick to your style

Try to avoid mixing styles in any element of design. This looks untidy, confused and disjointed, and is difficult to follow.

Centred

An interesting variation is to centre each line of type. When used in conjunction with a centred heading, this gives a strong, symmetrical appearance.

Rag right

As a variation, type can be aligned on the right of the measure. This has limited use because we are used to reading type from left to right; if too many lines are set in this style, the text can be hard to read.

Style

Make your decision before you start work and then stick to it. You will find it far easier to achieve a stylish, clear design.

▶ **Line measure**

Make sure you choose a line measure (or width) that suits the page format. Go for short measures on a portrait format and longer measures on a landscape format. Fit the type size to the measure.

Short measures
look better on a
portrait format.

Do not use long measures on a portrait format.

▼ **Explore different methods**

You can use many different and interesting styles of setting text. Don't be afraid to experiment until you find the style best suited to your scrapbook page.

Landscape formats allow wider measures to be used.

It came from
outer space

Irregular shapes are easy
to achieve with
computer setting. They
will add visual interest
to a piece of text and at
the same time they can
reflect the contents.

It came from
outer space

Irregular shapes are easy
to achieve with computer
setting. They will add
visual interest to a
piece of text and
at   the   same
time they can
reflect   the
contents.

It came from
OUTER SPACE

Irregular shapes are easy to achieve
with computer setting. They will add
visual interest to a piece of text
and can reflect the
contents.

STYLES OF LETTERING

Lettering for your titles and journaling can be created in a number of ways. You can use handwriting or computer fonts, create ornate lettering using calligraphy and decorative techniques such as stamping, or you can use title embellishments such as stickers and plaques.

Whatever style and technique you use for your lettering, remember to consider how it will work with the rest of your page. Does the colour go well with the background? Is the lettering legible? Does the style fit with the theme and feel of the page? Don't be afraid to experiment and consider a range of different lettering for each page.

Title embellishments

Alphabet embellishments are available in a wide range of stickers, plaques and rub-ons. You can also use more unusual embellishments, such as jigsaw puzzle shapes or bottle tops.

Lettering techniques

Books on calligraphy are widely available and the various styles can be recreated on your pages using a range of tools, from markers and pens to paints and glitter.

Using computer fonts

Once you start looking you will find that there is a huge range of fonts readily available to you – a number will come already installed on your computer, graphics programs usually come with even more, and on the internet there is a seemingly never-ending supply, some free, some for purchase. Your choice of font, especially for the title, will greatly influence the 'feel' of the page – whether fun, serious, romantic or nostalgic. As a scrapbooker, it is perfectly acceptable to use a number of different fonts on a page, though care must be taken with their choice, as some tend to go together better than others. When choosing a journaling font, in particular, take great care that it is easy to read – a very fancy font in blocks is tiring on the eye.

The following fonts are just a selection of some of the most popular and fun fonts available.

abcdefghijklmnopqrstuvwxyz

Bradley Hand (Galapagos Design Work)
This is a lovely handwriting font, very easy to read, and neat and attractive – great for journaling.

Camelot Caps (House of Lime)
This elegant font is beautiful for the capital letters of a title or monogram.

abcdefghijklmnopqrstuvwxyz

Century Gothic (Monotype Classic Fonts)
This formal and classic font is beautiful in a title or for journaling.

abcdefghijklmnopqrstuvwxyz

Dominican (Harold's Fonts)

Typewriter fonts have a charm all of their own, and this is an extremely charming font. With its old-world charm it is extremely good on heritage pages, and being easy to read makes it very suitable for journaling.

abcdefghijklmnopqrstuvwxyz

P22 Cezanne (P22)

This beautiful handwriting font (modelled on the writing of the artist, Paul Cézanne) is beautiful for titles, and lovely when used at low opacity as a background, for accent words in journaling.

abcdefghijklmnopqrstuvwxyz

DSP Curley Q Solid (Suzanne C Walker)

Curly fonts add a touch of playfulness, fun, funkiness and whimsy to a layout – and this is one of the nicest. If you use Photoshop, try adding a metal layer style to make wire-looking text.

abcdefghijklmnopqrstuvwxyz

Penstyle (IMSI MasterFonts)

A neat and attractive script is always useful. A script like this works extremely well in a traditional layout and can be used for either titles or journaling.

abcdefghijklmnopqrstuvwxyz

DSP Jamie (Suzanne C Walker)

Handwriting fonts always give a lovely handcrafted look to a layout – and with computer fonts you have the advantage of being able to edit and delete text before printing.

ABCDEFGHI JKLMNOPQRSTUVWXYZ

Punch Label

So often a scrapbook page needs a label, and this font will make a label for you, beautifully.

abcdefghijklmnopqrstuvwxyz

DSP Old General Store (Suzanne C Walker)

This lovely font, probably most useful for titles, has wonderful vintage charm, blending the old with the new in a delightful way; it also works well on a funky layout.

abcdefghijklmnopqrstuvwxyz

Scriptina (Apostrophic Labs)

This beautiful script, with its generous and graceful curves, is a favourite of many scrapbookers and makes wonderful titles.

abcdefghijklmnopqrstuvwxyz

Earwig Factory (Larabie Fonts)

This is definitely a fun font – and perfect for accenting words. Use a plain font, like Century Gothic, for the main journaling for effective contrast.

ABCDEFGHIJKLMNOPQRSTUVWXYZ

Stamp Act (Harold's Fonts)

No scrapbook font collection is complete without a good grungy, stamped-looking font. Stamp Act is a great titling font.

USING MANY PHOTOGRAPHS

When you start scrapbooking, the backlog of photographs that you face can seem quite daunting. Once your photographs have been sorted and organised, however, you may find that you have a range of photos that you could scrapbook in a number of different ways. The single shot that captures the essence of the occasion will work really well on its own on a page. On the other hand, what about those many snapshots that are not particularly stunning but that you still wish to use because they are an important reflection of your life?

Designing pages that include more than one or two photographs can be a challenge, so in these next few pages we offer you a number of design examples for using from one to ten photographs on the same page. These have been designed to offer you inspiration – they can be recreated exactly as shown here or you can use them as a springboard to your own creations.

Tip

The sketches accompanying each scrapbook page highlight the key design elements that make up the layout. Try rotating or flipping the sketches to produce new combinations that can be translated directly onto your album pages.

USING ONE PHOTOGRAPH

Bringing life to your pages

This photograph is packed with character. The image is simple, but strong and energetic – a great choice for a single page. Follow the eyes, look at that smile, and you can almost hear the laughter.

Use muted colours and patterns for a frame and background to emphasise a single image. Setting the picture at an angle, and layering it on a smaller, straight-on square of paper, makes it bounce off the page.

Pick up on a theme by using a key word for a bold effect – different-sized characters, set at slightly varying heights and angles, give a feeling of movement. Just like the baby, the page is bouncing with energy, so limit the colours, and keep them pale to avoid overpowering the design. Finally, soft pencil is good for writing in a personal comment – a secret memory, anecdote, or simply the day and date add to the atmosphere.

USING TWO PHOTOGRAPHS

Using boyish embellishments

Select complementary subjects to pick out a special theme. Pictures that express the same sentiment in a slightly different way go well together. A pair of similar snaps are more striking when they are just slightly different in angle and proportion. This is the way to capture and secure the feeling of the moment. Overlap photographs to minimise less-interesting background areas.

A monochrome or single-colour background in a cool shade will look tranquil. Pick out natural forms from photographs for design features. The light and shade of calm water is represented in this background, making the most of the muted green and blue in the pictures. Boyish embellishments, such as natural twine or string, knotted rather than in bows, tie the theme in with the images.

Colourful and bold effect

When a pair of photographs has a subject looking out to camera, place them so that they are facing in the same direction. Having them 'back to back' would look awkward.

It's a good idea to pick out garment styles as well as natural fabrics on your page design. For example, the shoulder straps on this little boy's outfit are reflected in the three hanging buckles and the band of loose-weave fabric underneath.

This is a colourful scene, full of down-to-earth activity, which is represented in the slightly chunky, quite busy embellishments. Tough-looking trimmings can be graphic rather than pretty, and very stylish. All texture and shape, and no words, work well on some pages.

USING THREE PHOTOGRAPHS

Zooming in on detail

When taking photographs of precious items, remember to zoom in to capture details. Position a detailed photograph carefully – here, the shoes look better at the feet-end of the page rather than off to one side, or at head height.

Strips of fairly plain paper link photographs well, and top and bottom borders will enclose the page. Clean lines or muted background patterns can reflect the picture content – on this page, the stripes pick out the shirt fabric.

To prevent the eye from following a line off the page, add a clever device that leads back to the main subject. A zig-zag of fabric or paper works well. It is also easy to copy and paste a pattern from a photograph on the computer, then print it and cut out strips. Fix the zig-zag on a wide mount with one of the pictures so it relates well and attracts attention.

Different textures and materials

Use strong textures to throw out images. Different materials can be married – try metal, leather, buckles, ribbon, and paper. They work here to balance the sepia monochrome, rather than colour, photographs.

Using photographs taken from roughly the same angle, vary the proportions for a flowing layout. The smaller image here is a detail of the bride's expression.

Use different frames to emphasise different images – a small, close and feminine frame works around a female portrait; a torn-page style works on the frame with journaling detail; and a fine white border with a couple of corner embellishments can replace a frame completely. Bold lettering in a decorative style will enhance and complete a page.

USING FOUR PHOTOGRAPHS

Minimum colour for maximum impact

We all take lots of photos of the same scene, especially when there's a new baby or when it's a special occasion, such as Christmas. It's a good idea to focus on two sizes of photographs, with one centrepiece, when the subject poses are very similar. Keep clean lines with plain backgrounds, and a limited colour palette for maximum impact.

Position thumbnail pictures at complementary angles to anchor the big subject. Hide corners of repeated detail (for example, one hand) with a small picture. A black mount enhances the main subject.

Stamping is a good technique for adding festive features. Add a little glitter and a Christmas-style flower. Festive lettering is traditional and 'homely' and contrasts well.

Using letters to unite pictures

Cut out hard card to frame a collection of complementary, but different, photographs. Close-up pictures can be quite intense, so try balancing them with one that is distant and less detailed. Soft colours ensure that the focus is not taken away from the four shots, and a tiny print used for part of the background can be repeated on one frame.

When opting for a busy, and quite distinctive, pattern in the background, it's a good idea to keep embellishments to a minimum. Fine ribbon, little bows or cut-out hearts complement the baby theme – but take care not to overdo it.

Bold but soft, plain letters are a good choice for a title. Splitting the title across the page can be a good way of uniting the pictures, leading the eye from the top and across to the bottom of the page.

USING FIVE PHOTOGRAPHS

Using space

Christmas trimmings and photographs of decorating the tree revive memories. Photographs do not have to be large to make an impact; instead, keep them small and equal in size. Create a simple layout when using five busy pictures. Allow detail and action in the photographs to dominate.

Leave plenty of space to balance the busy pictures, providing the eye with restful areas, and keep the title, and comment, to a minimum. Sometimes, a familiar phrase in stark lettering works well, especially when pale characters stand out on a dark background. Add a narrow patterned border to ensure that the page does not look too stark. Using soft lettering for dates is also a good way of capturing the slightly illusive quality of seasonal celebration.

Capture a moment, not a pose

Remember to take lots of photos on special occasions. Weddings are packed with personal details – the flowers, cake, table settings, invitations, decorations, clothes, gifts... Use different settings, as well as the usual formal situations.

On your pages, reflect the colours and textures of the day. Try using one picture large, and four small but similar in size. The large picture does not have to be a traditional pose – a close-up of an 'active' photo can be beautiful. The bride's hands and ring are classic themes that are often shown in a rather rigid setting, but they look good in a natural pose. Aim to capture the moment.

Flowing lettering looks good on labels that break into the edges of the main picture. Fine ribbon is perfect for linking the images – especially if it is ribbon saved from the wedding itself.

USING SIX PHOTOGRAPHS

Using supporting shots

Transform a potentially plain sequence of similar images into a brilliant background for an extended title. Select a stunning photograph to fill a large proportion of the page. When the expression of the person in the picture says it all, let it steal the show! Pick out a series of supporting shots that confirm the mood and use them as a base for your lettering. Spell out the theme in words, phrases or ideas, and print them on acetate.

Keep background colour and pattern to a minimum for a stylish and modern design. Fix the pictures simply – ribbon and eyelets are good for securing acetate over photographs. Tilt the style towards the theme with one or two finishing touches – no more or the page will be cluttered. A favourite flower, a charm, odd earring or bead would be ideal.

Cut and paste a panorama

Recreate a panoramic scene by using a series of five photographs. Instead of trying to match them perfectly, make a feature of the sections by overlapping and tilting the prints. To achieve the casual – but highly successful – look, ensure you print the photo multiple times. Play with different positions, angles and overlaps until the sequence is just right.

A plain but strong colour works well as a background. Text printed out and cut as fine tape can make a casual, but distinct, base line to hold the pictures in place. Layering is a good way of presenting a title, focusing on just one or two words, such as a place name. A simple border pattern along the bottom of a page emphasises a tall, vertical image. Add a sixth photograph (a long shot of the image) mounted on a colour to pick up the border and complete the page. Try a vertical title strapline or border on horizontal or landscape images.

USING SEVEN PHOTOGRAPHS

Lead your subject out of the page

Photo-manipulation software can be used to write in a style that matches words on patterned paper. The phrases can be overprinted on a photograph. Try pairing images in a sequence of six small photographs, and overlap them to reduce repetitive background, drawing attention to the action. Complement action-packed pictures with a more reflective, calm image.

Instead of squaring up a large photograph, tilt the background to give more movement. Arranging the photograph so that the subject appears to be reading the title on the page – or is about to pick up one of the embellishments – is a clever technique for anchoring the image and drawing together the whole page, while keeping it 'active' rather than passive.

Mix styles

Several different formats of photograph, and design styles, can work well on the same page. When there is some restful space in a large main image – for example, a large proportion of water (as here) – the supporting pictures, or different styles of text, can be busy without making the layout too cluttered.

Keep the photo border even on three sides, and then overlap small images along the fourth edge. As well as squared-off pictures, try using cut-outs on a plain background.

Try using rub-ons directly on your photograph for an elaborate title, especially with a unique choice of words. Decorative corner pieces are great for picking up on architectural or cultural themes, and overlapping them on pictures can anchor different elements on a page. Handwritten notes are useful for recording personal memories.

Moments of **Perfection**

VENICE

A city of mirrors, a city of mirages at once solid and liquid; at once air and stone. a city filled with moments of perfection

July 2005

USING EIGHT PHOTOGRAPHS

Ample border for a busy montage

If you have an APS camera and receive an index print card, have a go at using these on your scrapbook page. For example, the index print images can be used on a tag, as here, to include lots of fun images that could become boring when used large.

Instead of spreading out a large number of photographs, it's sometimes a good idea to keep them in a tight arrangement in the middle of the page. The large areas of water in the pictures have been cropped out, but the plain blue page border is wide, and it gets the poolside message across.

The lettering jigs about for fun, while contrasting circles in the mounting reflect those first bubbling, burbling water experiences!

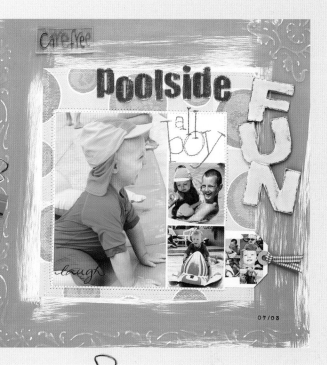

Creating movement

The nuances of real-life scenery can be lost in a stack of photographs, so look for clever ways to make the images interesting. By using different size photographs you can get lots more on the page, and cropping will make them more exciting.

This scrapbooker shows how to make the most of co-ordinating stickers to create a hidden journaling folder. Small buttons, thread and tags co-ordinate well. Dark and light backgrounds against individual letters keeps the title moving, as does a strapline across the page.

The colour, texture and pace in the way the pictures are used – looking at the view over the shoulder of the subject, or following someone pointing out detail – give a feeling of rough travel. Notice how different this is from sophisticated city pages.

USING NINE PHOTOGRAPHS

Capturing personality

Do you have lots of photos that are more or less the same? Using them passport size, and displaying them on strips of real negative is a good way of showcasing them. It's a great way of capturing slightly different facial expressions. Bold numerals in different sizes make a background that has a 'growing up' feel about it; breaking it up with a frayed-edge band along the bottom prevents it from becoming too dominant.

Messages and titles can be added to tags and ties. Getting a masculine page just right means playing with different type styles and colours. Use trimmings and finishing touches that are plain, and they won't look too fussy.

Limited picture shapes and sizes

It's easy to create a scrapbook page using nine photographs – just crop them to fit. The trick is to select a limited number of shapes and sizes, and stick to them. Small square pictures fit with tall rectangles. Have a key image to 'take control' of the page, and hold all the smaller photographs together. Keeping the photographs in two or three groups, rather than having them all over the pages, ensures that the layout is not cluttered.

While the same pose works on a series of small pictures, select different angles for larger shots. Arrange them to create the impression of the person turning around on the page. Add subtle curves or circles for contrast.

Light on dark works well when the photographs are mounted on dark card.

USING TEN PHOTOGRAPHS

Using a strong background

Same suit, different child... show off your children on the same page by using this clean and simple style. Matching one large picture with a strip of negative-style shots is a classic and successful design technique. It's also a great way of getting lots of 'everyday' images of growing children together. There's lots to look at, comparisons to be made, and having to study the negative strips makes this page more interesting.

Avoid over-doing the trimmings. Reversing out characters from a black background makes them stand out. Outline characters with seasonal 'snow' are fun but not fussy. The Christmas greeting is traditional, and because it is quite different in style from the pictures and other lettering, it does not become too 'busy'. A little gift and tag completes the decoration.

Using colour

Black-and-white photographs can be repeated to make stunning pages. Remember not to use too many different sizes – for example, opt for three settings. Boxing is a good method to start building up the arrangement. Enlarge one image and print it in colour too. Not all the photographs need mounting or framing – a combination of mounted, framed and unframed can work. Trim the edges of photographs if you want them to bleed off the edges of your pages – for example, at the corners, to get rid of excess plain background.

A feminine page does not have to be pink and full of petals! Muted shades and one little bow highlight the softness. Letters in different sizes, set slightly out of line and tilt, give the impression that the subject is fun and informal.

DIGITAL SCRAPBOOKING

Digital scrapbooking is a no-mess, time-saving alternative to conventional scrapbooking. Photo-manipulation programs (see pages 42-43) allow you to carry out a multitude of neat tricks with your photographs, including cropping, changing colours and duplicating images. In the same way, digital scrapbooking programs allow you to experiment and try out new ideas without damaging your photographs or pages – if you mess up at any time, you can simply hit the 'undo' button, which takes you straight back to where you were before. You can also make multiple copies of a page, and post your pages via email, or show them on the Web.

Digital scrapbooking online

There are several websites that can tell you more about digital scrapbooking, many of which include free tutorials and software downloads. A great site to start with is **www.digitalscrapbookplace.com**

HOW TO GET STARTED

Put your photographs on your computer

If you have a digital camera this is easy. You can download your photos from your camera to your computer using the instructions that came with your particular camera. If you don't have a digital camera, you will need a scanner to scan them in.

Choose your software – a layout or photo-manipulation program

Layout programs allow you to assemble pre-made graphics, photos, and journaling for quick scrapbook layouts. However, many layout programs do not meet the criteria that digital scrapbookers need. Either they don't support transparent PNG files, they are not capable of at least 200ppi (pixels per inch) for quality printing, or they do not

have the ability to place shadows. Choose your software carefully. A photo-manipulation program, such as Adobe Photoshop or Adobe Photoshop Elements, can also be used. There are more powerful programs, but these are more complicated to use.

Create your scrapbook pages

Photo-manipulation programs should come with full instructions or you can sign up for online tutorials. You may want to use digital page kits when you first begin – these can be downloaded or ordered on CD. They come with ready-to-use layouts and themed background papers and elements, such as digital versions of stamps, stickers, fibres, frames and all other embellishments that you could wish to use.

▼ Using computers, you can produce impressive pages and effects unlike anything achievable with conventional scrapbooking.

RESOLUTION

When working with digital images, you need to be sure that the picture is saved at the correct resolution. At the top of the dialogue under 'document size' verify that the photo is at least 200ppi and several inches in size. If the layout is 8x10 inches (20x25cm) at 200ppi, then the photo should be roughly the same size and resolution.

Most digital cameras take high quality photos at 300ppi, and low (web) quality photos at 72ppi. If you take photos at low quality, they won't be suitable for printing. Change the camera settings to take print-quality photographs.

Save as you go

Most scrapbookers save their pages in one of three different ways:

1 *In the native format of their program. This will keep all layers intact in case you ever need to go back and change anything (names, typos, photos and so on).*

2 *As a high resolution (200–300ppi) JPEG for easy printing. For this option, merge all layers, choose 'save as' and then save as a JPEG with very little compression.*

3 *As a low resolution (72ppi) JPEG for the web; 432 pixels tall is a good size for easy screen viewing. You can adjust the compression to make your image under 125K, which is the limit on most websites.*

Using a tools palette

Photoshop has become the most common graphics and painting package. Most Photoshop basics are applicable to other image-manipulation software, so what you learn here will be useful elsewhere.

1 Marquee tools

Used to select areas of an image defined by the shape of the tool.

2 Lasso tools

These allow you to select areas of the image while allowing greater freedom in defining the shape of your selection.

3 Crop tool

Used to trim an image down, removing unwanted parts.

4 Clone stamp

This is mostly useful when editing photographs.

5 Eraser

Deletes areas of the image according to the thickness and edge of the brush size selected – effectively, the Paintbrush in reverse. If you use this on the base layer (or 'background') it will use your secondary colour.

6 Vector path tools

These are advanced tools for creating curved shapes and selections that can be scaled up to any size without pixelating. They can be difficult to use but create smooth, curved areas.

7 Magic wand

This tool selects an area of the image based on the shapes and lines of the existing image.

8 Pencil mode

This applies colour with a sharp, pixelated edge rather than a soft, translucent one. It is the best way to ensure a perfectly crisp edge to your line areas.

9 Text tool

Use this to place text on the page. Click on the page to create a text line, and hold down the mouse button and drag to create a multiline text box with wrapping text.

10 Eyedropper

The eyedropper tool samples colour from the image and automatically changes the current colour to the newly sampled selection.

11 Zoom tool

Allows you to zoom in and out of the image, making it larger or smaller on screen. You can also use the Ctrl + [–] and Ctrl + [+] keys to do this.

CREATING A DIGITAL SCRAPBOOK PAGE STEP BY STEP

Creating a digital scrapbook page is easy once you have mastered the basic techniques of your chosen program. This scrapbooker has used Adobe Photoshop to create a simple display page for her vacation. Once you have learnt how to manipulate photographs and play with text, you can begin to create exciting and inventive pages.

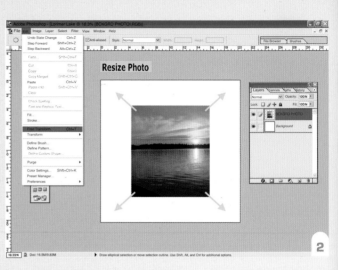

Resize Photo

2

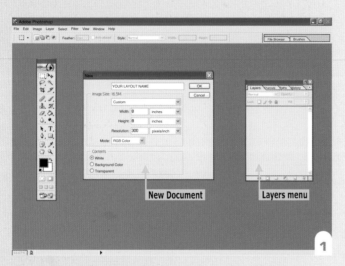

New Document

Layers menu

1

1 Click FILE > NEW to create a new document that measures 8x8 inches (20x20cm) with a resolution of 300dpi (dots per inch) and a white background. Ensure layers menu is showing (if not, click WINDOW > LAYERS).

2 Select a photograph (or papers) you would like to use as a background. Open this image and drag it to your new page, or use the copy and paste functions. Click EDIT > FREE TRANSFORM to resize the image to fit the page.

Elliptical Marquee Tool

3

3 Select photographs to accent your background. Drag and drop or cut and paste these photos onto your new page. To crop them into circles, use the ELLIPTICAL MARQUEE TOOL and hold down shift while dragging to get a perfect circle. Position over the area you wish to crop, click SELECT > INVERSE and press DELETE. To resize photo, click EDIT > FREE TRANSFORM and hold down the shift key while dragging to keep the proportions constant.

relax

Lorimer Lake 2005

The finished page shows the sophisticated finish achievable with digital techniques.

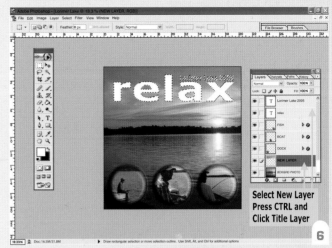

4 Position your accent photos and give them a bit of a lift by adding effects. Click LAYER > LAYER STYLE to display the effects menu. Here, bevel and emboss have been used for the three accent photos.

6 Make sure this new layer is selected in the layers menu and while pressing CTRL on the keyboard, click your title layer from the same menu (you will see the text selected). Click SELECT > INVERSE and press DELETE.

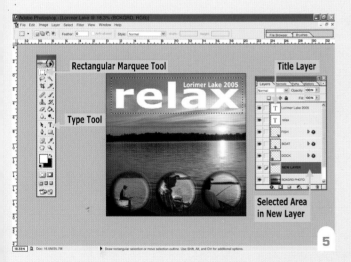

5 To make the title from part of the background, use the TYPE tool and click in the area you wish to place the type. With the RECTANGULAR MARQUEE tool, select the area around the word. Make sure you are on the background photo layer and click EDIT > COPY and EDIT > PASTE. This will create a new layer with the selected background area.

7 From the layers menu, make your title layer and background photo layer invisible (you will see the text filled with the selected part of the photo). To make the text visible on the background photo, add a drop shadow or use an effect like bevel and emboss.

OTHER SCRAPBOOK-RELATED PROJECTS

The skills and techniques used to create traditional scrapbook pages can also be used to produce beautiful keepsake projects that can be just as meaningful as a large-scale album. These tend to be specific to particular themes or events, and can be much faster to produce than an entire album. For this reason, this type of project can make the perfect gift.

▼ Papier mâché boxes

Papier mâché boxes are available together with concertina folded albums. These provide a fixed number of pages for you to decorate. The robust nature of papier mâché albums means that you can use bulkier embellishments than in a standard album. This can be creatively liberating, allowing you to incorporate more unusual elements. Painted and decorated, these boxed albums are beautiful in their own right and provide a protective environment for their contents.

▶ Brown paper bag books

Brown paper bags can be folded together to create the pages of a book. The openings of the bag are perfect pockets for additional pictures or journaling. The folded base of each bag can be separated to produce more pockets or folded and fastened to create secret pockets that make these books a joy to explore. Since paper bags are not completely archivally safe, either spray the bags first with an acid-neutralising spray or only use duplicate photographs.

Boxes and cans

Old boxes and cans make great containers for mini projects. Choose from tiny sweet cans to film canisters or paint cans. Crafters are using all of these to create stunning containers for albums made quickly and simply from cardstock. A collection of pages can be secured together with ribbons or fibres for a decorative and practical fastening. Creating an album in a can with decorated pages that leave spaces for the recipient's photographs is a wonderful way to share your scrapbooking skills.

TAG ART

The skills and techniques used to create scrapbook pages and, more particularly, tags to decorate these pages has led to an offshoot craft of 'tag art'. These tags can be incorporated into scrapbook layouts or stand alone as mini works of art. Using a simple postal tag as its base, a tag can become a clean and simple embellishment or a complex collage of artistic expression – the choice is yours.

You can also experiment with tag art to try new techniques. Use a variety of mediums for your tag base, from cardstock to wood, acrylic and even glass – remember that each material will respond differently to the techniques applied.

Hidden journaling

Tags can also be used to conceal journaling on your page. Decoratively cover one side of the tag while hiding your personal writing on the other side. Once attached to your page, the writing will be hidden to the casual viewer, but still accessible to you.

Tip

Try mixing techniques and styles on a tag to produce interesting effects – for example, try materials that you would not usually combine, such as metal and fabric.

Tag technique

A piece of map creates a beautiful base and a key-ring makes a great hanger for a travel-themed tag.

Thread formica chips together on a length of bead chain for a clean and simple collection of tags embellished with rub-ons.

Mix stamps and metal embellishments together on a painted tag for a romantic feel.

An eclectic collection of ephemera is showcased on a base of ultra-thick embossing enamel that has been stamped into.

Low-cost embellishments

An advantage of tag art is that it provides an opportunity to use up scraps of leftover materials, making it a low-cost way to produce embellishments. The small scale of a tag means that it does not require a lot of products to decorate it and it will encourage you to become more ingenious in your methods.

Tag book

The tags that are usually attached to a scrapbook page can also be attached together to create a series of pages in a mini album. A few scraps of ribbon, some charms and patterned paper can be combined with small-scale photographs to produce a unique and personal project.

Collage scraps of patterned paper together onto a tag to create a vintage-themed tag.

Create a marble effect on glossy card using alcohol inks. Teaming this with a beaded trim creates a romantic and eye-catching tag.

together forever

CHAPTER 5

THE ART OF JOURNALING

The pace of life is so fast today that it can be difficult to find the time to tell the stories relevant to the significant events of our lives. There is a real danger that our oral family history will be eroded. Journaling provides the opportunity to record these stories before they are lost.

Journaling is the story behind the pictures on your scrapbook pages. It tells the viewer the details that cannot always be conveyed by images alone. You can also choose to use journaling as a means of expressing yourself in a way that you may not otherwise be comfortable with. Journaling can be used as a way to express loss, sadness, love, joy and many other emotions — it does not have to be open for all to see, but what is important is that it is there.

7Gypsies

HOW TO TELL THE STORY

Journaling is the personal expression of the stories of your photographs, and can be as simple or as complex as you choose. These are your stories, after all, and there is no wrong way in which to do this.

Basic information

The most basic level of journaling will tell simply the names and dates relevant to the photos. 'Who?' and 'when?' are usually the first questions asked in relation to photographs and can be quickly and simply incorporated into your design, often in a basic heading such as 'Summer' or 'Family'.

Basic information

WHO *Mum and Joe*

WHEN *Summer 2005*

tip *Keep it simple for maximum effect*

Basic and secondary information

WHO *Ella*

WHEN *Spring 2005*

WHAT *Bon Jovi concert*

WHY *'Because I love Bon Jovi!'*

WHERE *Madison Square Garden*

Secondary information

More advanced journaling takes into account both basic and secondary information – not just 'who?' and 'when?' but also 'what?', 'why?' and 'where?'. Using these five questions as your guide will help you to incorporate the essential elements of journaling.

CREATIVE JOURNALING

Your journaling does not always need to give just basic facts – there are many other ways to journal your scrapbook pages.

You could try journaling in a list format – it is a quick way to get key words onto the page and gets straight to the point. Write your lists as bullet points to emphasise this style of journaling for a clean and crisp look.

Using the words of others can also help you to communicate your message – song lyrics, poetry and Bible passages are all great ways to bring thoughts and feelings into your pages (see Quotations, page 88).

It can also be easier to journal information that feels personal, and your memories and feelings will make a wonderful treasure for the future.

Proverbs 22:6
Teach a child to choose the right path, and when he is older, he will remain upon it.

Quotations
Quotations can o
provide the perfec
journaling for you
page or photograp
Here, the passage
from the Bible give
just the right
accompaniment to
this photograph.

Letters
You can use real letters for your journaling, or even just imagine that you are writing a letter to a specific person as a way of expressing your feelings. Using older letters is a great way of preserving them for the future.

1º, EARL'S COURT SQUA
TEL. FLAXMAN 8800.

Dear Mom,

Thank you so much for the beaut
for William for his birthday. It fits h
has not taken it off all week!

Much love,
Peter

Peter Humphreys

Our family brownie recipe
4 large eggs
1 cup sugar, sifted
1 cup brown sugar, sifted
8 ounces melted butter
1¼ cups cocoa, sifted
2 teaspoons vanilla extract
½ cup flour, sifted
½ teaspoon salt

Recipes and family memorabilia
This cherished family recipe makes great journaling for this photograph, and ensures that it is recorded for others to use.

HOW TO WRITE IN AN ENGAGING WAY

You may decide you want to elaborate on the factual information in your journaling and write your own narrative about your photographs. If you do, you will need to take into account the way in which you tell your story.

These two passages (right) tell the same story, but the second version is far more effective. They are both the same length, but the second draft contains more detail and reads more fluently. Cross-refer between the two examples, noting the following points: At (A) in the first passage there is a lack of necessary detail – who was her first husband? The same applies at (B) and (C) where the reader will want to know what kind of house and how much older John Smith was. At (D) the sentence is needlessly passive – it reads better to say that John Smith 'wrote the letters' rather than that they 'were written by' him. At (E) the reference to the date of birth is accurate, but saying something happened on Boxing Day or St Stephen's Day is far more evocative than merely using the date. The words used at (F) are too flowery and distract from the story rather than adding to it. The sentence at (G) is both passive and lacking in available detail. The words used at (H) are again too flowery and pretentious, and they strike the wrong note.

1st draft

Maria Smith, who had been married before (A), loved her new husband John. She made their house in Boston (B) into a real home. In turn, John Smith, who was older than Maria (C), was a devoted husband. According to letters written by him (D) to his cousin Ernest, which have survived to this day, the five years that he was married to Maria were the happiest of his life. In one of them he wrote: 'It never fails to amaze me how the love of a good person like Maria can be such a great source of comfort and security. I never realised that one could be so content with life'. John Smith was even happier when Maria gave birth to a son, whom they called Albert John, on 26 December 1898 (E).

Alas, the blissful, joyous idyll that constituted John Smith's life did not last long (F). A serious disease claimed Maria's life (G) just eighteen months later on 17 June 1900 after a long illness. She was just twenty-seven. John was distraught, and within a year of his wife's death had moved back to Albany, the place that he had left at the age of sixteen. There are few records of what John did over the next few years. All that the dusty, moth-eaten annals of historic records inform us with any certainty (H) is that he died on 11 May 1906 and that his son Albert was the sole remaining survivor of John Smith's immediate family.

Revised draft

Maria Smith, who had previously been married to a gambling and philandering tailor called Paul Jones (A), loved her new husband John. She made their tiny little house, a former draper's shop in the Boston suburbs (B), into a real home. In turn John Smith, who was sixteen years older than Maria (C), was a devoted husband. According to letters that he wrote to his cousin Ernest (D), which have survived to this day, the five years he was married to Maria were the happiest of his life. In one of them he wrote: 'It never fails to amaze me how the love of a good person like Maria can be such a wonderful source of comfort and security. I never realized that one could be so content with life'. John Smith was even happier when Maria gave birth to a son, whom they called Albert John, on Boxing Day 1898 (E).

Sadly, John Smith's contented life did not last long (F). Maria died of tuberculosis just eighteen months later (G), on 17 June 1900, after a long illness. She was just twenty-seven. John was distraught, and within a year of his wife's death had moved back to Albany, the place he had left at the age of sixteen. There are few records of what John did over the next few years. All we know for sure (H) is that he died on 11 May 1906 and that his son Albert was the sole remaining survivor of the family.

INCLUDING HANDWRITING

Your handwriting is a personal expression of who you are. It can give a glimpse into your education and background, and aspects of your personality. There is something special about finding handwritten letters, recipes and notes from previous generations – something that is becoming increasingly rare in our own time.

Try to include an example of your handwriting somewhere in your album, regardless of whether you like it or not. Also consider including the handwriting of the subjects of your pages. The writing of children changes as they develop and can provide fun memories. Friends and relatives may like to write notes to capture a story from their perspective.

▶ HANDWRITING OR TYPE?

Handwriting will always be appreciated as a simple and effective way of adding that extra personal element to your pages – but it is important not to forget that computer-generated text can offer a wider range of fonts, sizes and colours. When deciding the best way to add your journaling, you should explore every option available to you.

Tip

Remember that in order to preserve handwriting, it should be written with an archival pen, using inks that have been tested for longevity. Archival pens are also safer to use with your photographs.

Which pen?

There is a wide range of different pens and markers available to use for your journaling, many of which have been created specifically for scrapbooking. Shop around and consider what kind of line, style and colour you want your writing to be displayed in.

◀ **Fountain pens**
Fountain pens have interchangeable broad-edged tips of different sizes and their own reservoir of ink. They are great for producing an elegant, refined effect.

▶ **Calligraphy markers**
Calligraphy markers have a broad-edged tip, and come in a range of tip widths labeled in millimetres.

◀ **Marker pens**
Marker pens come in a variety of thicknesses and colours, and are easy to use.

Using handwriting

The handwriting on this page renders the already personal message more meaningful, in a way that type would not.

Using type

The advantages of using type include neatness and legibility, as well as a wide range of different styles and colours. However, that personal touch is often sacrificed in the process.

Personal messages

This scrapbooker has included a personal message on her page for her son to read in years to come. These words of wisdom are all the more precious and unique for being written in the scrapbooker's own handwriting.

Preserving your handwriting

It is now possible to have your handwriting converted into a font at relatively low cost. A handwriting font offers all the flexibility and accuracy of a word processing font, while still maintaining some of the characteristics of your own personal style. It also preserves your handwriting for future generations.

Original handwriting

the quick brown fox

Handwriting converted to font

the quick brown fox

QUOTATIONS

Sometimes the words of others are just right for expressing your sentiments. Quotations can be used as a title or as journaling for your pages, capturing the feeling and theme of your pictures quickly and simply.

Quotations can come from many different places – from books and films to songs and television shows. You can use extracts from all kinds of written and unwritten material – just be sure to give credit to the original author.

FINDING QUOTATIONS ON THE INTERNET

There are a number of great resources for finding useful quotations. You can start by searching the internet. There are a whole host of websites that specialise in quotations and famous sayings. You can find anything from poems to film quotations just by undertaking a simple search. Entering a specific word will produce quotations that are specifically relevant to your page and theme. Searching each site for a word or phrase will speed up the process of finding the perfect quotation – and the more words you use in your search, the more specific the results will be.

Try out the following websites:

www.quotationspage.com
www.twopeasinabucket.com/peasoup.asp
www.quotemountain.com

Wise words

HAPPINESS

When times are good be happy.
Ecclesiastes, ch 7, v 14

Being content is as good as an endless feast.
Proverbs, ch 15, v 15

Be thou the rainbow in the storms of life. The evening beam that smiles the clouds away, and tints tomorrow with prophetic ray.
Byron

Laughter is the brush that sweeps away the cobwebs of the heart.
Mort Walker

Consult not your fears but your hopes and your dreams. Think not about your frustrations, but about your unfulfilled potential. Concern yourself not with what you tried and failed in, but with what it is still possible for you to do.
Pope John XXIII

There are always flowers for those who want to see them.
Henri Matisse

ANIMALS

What greater gift than the love of a cat?
Charles Dickens

Animals are such agreeable friends – they ask no questio they pass no criticisms.
George Eliot

A dog is the only thing on earth that loves you more than he loves himself.
Josh Billings

Dogs come when they're called; cats take a message and get back to you later.
Mary Bly

BABIES AND CHILDREN

A new baby is like the beginning of all things – wonder, hope, a dream of possibilities.
Eda J. Le Shan

When the first baby laughed for the first time, the laugh broke into a thousand pieces and they all went skipping about, and that was the beginning of fairies. And now when every new baby is born its first laugh becomes a fairy.
J.M. Barrie

Children are the bridge to heaven.
Persian Proverb

The smallest children are nearest to God, as the smallest planets are nearest the sun.
Jean Paul Richter

Children learn to smile from their parents.
Shinichi Suzuk

Allow children to be happy in their own way, for what better way will they find?
Samuel Johnson

The finest inheritance you can give to a child is to allow it to make its own way, completely on its own feet.
Isadora Duncan

LOVE

In dreams and in love there are no impossibilities.
Janos Arany

Where there is love there is life.
Indira Gandhi

To say the truth, reason and love keep little company together nowadays.
William Shakespeare

So fall asleep love, loved by me ... for I know love, I am loved by thee.
Robert Browning

A happy marriage has in it all the pleasures of friendship, all the enjoyments of sense and reason, and indeed, all the sweets of life.
Joseph Addison

FRIENDSHIP

Life has no pleasure higher or nobler than that of friendship.
Samuel Johnson

Friendship is a sheltering tree.
Samuel Taylor Coleridge

Promise me you'll always remember: you're braver than you believe, and stronger than you seem, and smarter than you think.
A.A. Milne

Don't let grass grow on the path of friendship.
Indian Proverb

Don't walk in front of me; I may not follow. Don't walk behind me; I may not lead. Just walk beside me and be my friend.
Albert Camus

The friendship that can cease has never been real.
St Jerome

Friendship redoubleth joys, and cutteth griefs in half.
Francis Bacon

HIDDEN JOURNALING

Hidden journaling is the term for literally hiding writing on a page. It is used for many reasons – to conceal private thoughts that you want to include but not show to many people; to prevent bad handwriting from spoiling the look of a page; or to include a story or thought conceived after the page is completed.

Hinges

You can conceal your journaling by writing it onto the back of a photograph or photo mount. Then attach the picture to your layout using hinges or photo flips – these conceal the writing, but allow it to be revealed when wished.

Take care to use an archival pen to ensure that your journaling will last and not damage your precious pictures. Do not press too hard when writing onto the reverse side of photos as this can emboss through to the front. Use a hard surface to minimise the risk of imprinting onto the front of your photos.

The simplest method

The most obvious way of hiding your journaling is by writing it onto the back of your layout. Dark-coloured cardstock can be difficult to write on, but this can be done with a white or silver pen. Dark-paper pens are available specifically designed to write onto dark colours, and are available in a number of colours.

Tip

If you want to add a lengthy piece of journaling, it can be folded and placed in an envelope."

POCKETS AND ENVELOPES

For accessible hidden journaling, write onto tags or cards, and then slip these into pockets or envelopes. There are many different types and styles of journaling pockets available – or you might want to make one using a template like those shown here.

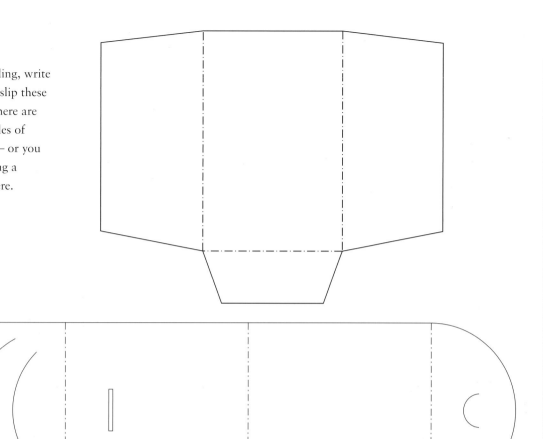

Using envelopes

By creating a vellum envelope for her journaling, this scrapbooker is tempting the viewer to investigate further. This journaling can be easily read by pulling it out using the clip holding it.

MEMORABILIA

The memorabilia of your life – the tickets, letters, certificates, coins and so on – can be like little pieces of treasure that you want to keep. Most of us end up keeping these items hidden away in a box or a drawer, and only rarely look at them. However, such memorabilia can be incorporated into your scrapbooks, and can be used to make a page really special. Your precious memories are then more easily accessible, and included with relevant photographs, while being preserved in the best possible archival environment.

USING MEMORABILIA WITH CARE

Printed materials are rarely printed on acid-free paper and some items can be too bulky to incorporate onto a scrapbook page. To protect your pictures, while still preserving and making use of your memorabilia, there are steps you can take to minimise the risk of deterioration or damage.

SPRAY: *Neutralise the acid in paper-based memorabilia by applying an archival spray.*

SEAL: *Protect the photographs on your page by sealing memorabilia away from harm. Place into specifically designed pockets or envelopes or laminate items using archivally safe products.*

SCAN: *Large or bulky items can be scanned and the image reduced in scale to fit onto your page.*

SNAP: *Unusually shaped or bulky memorabilia can be photographed to transform it into a medium that can be used on your page.*

Memories remembered

Certificates and records of achievement

These items can be used on pages together with photographs of the event to create a comprehensive memento of the occasion.

Holiday souvenirs

Memorabilia of your holidays can include everything from train and plane tickets to sand and shells collected on the beach. These can all be used to accentuate your holiday scrapbook pages.

Special outings

Special outings and events, such as big concerts, or even a memorable trip to the movies can be recorded and remembered by keeping and using the tickets on your pages.

The Blackpool Tower
Valid on 05 Aug 2005
NO CIRCUS
After Circus Evening
£8.00

GREEN DAY
PLUS SPECIAL
SUNDAY 1
JUNE 200
NATIONAL
BOWL
MILTON
KEYNES

SPONGEBOB SQU
2   F   6
14/02/05   12.15
ODEON

Children's drawings

The cards and drawings that children produce are wonderful and make great treasures. Incorporate them into your pages to preserve them safely for the future.

Public record

Sometimes the events of your life might be recorded in a more public way – an article in the local community paper perhaps. If treated in the right way, the fragile newspaper can be preserved to keep a permanent memory of your moment of fame.

SCOUTS' SHOW SHOULD DRAW TALENT SCOUTS

THERE'S something produced by switching about a scout show that channels. It's the first time I've compels audience partici- seen the ideas attempted ...tion South London on stage and the result was a slick performance with worthy of professional ...rtists.

Medals and badges

Medals and badges are not only precious mementos, but they can also be used as great embellishments, preserving them while also adding a special touch to your pages.

Mementos of growth

Memorabilia of a child's growth and development is something that all parents keep, and want to preserve, for the memories that they will bring back later in life. All the little things that you keep – hair from a first haircut, first teeth, first shoes – can all be used on your pages.

TECHNIQUES

Once you are familiar with the basic principles of scrapbooking – how to use photographs, design pages and include journaling – you can then begin to focus on learning and using the specific craft techniques that form an essential part of scrapbooking.

These pages take you through basic, textural and colouring techniques, from die cuts, stamping and embossing to using sewing, beads, chalks and paints. Each technique is accompanied by detailed step-by-step instructions, so you can follow the procedure at each stage. Finished examples then show the techniques in the context of professionally-produced scrapbook pages – these are accompanied by diagramatic devices, which isolate the key compositional and layout devices used, making it easier for you to copy or adapt the schemes.

CARD & PAPER

Cardstock and patterned paper will form the foundation of your scrapbook pages, and they are available in a rainbow of colours to suit all styles and themes of photographs. Cardstock is also available in a variety of textures and thickness that respond differently to a range of techniques. Look out for those that are double sided, embossed or textured, to add extra interest to your designs.

Materials

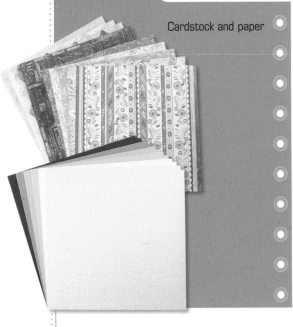

Cardstock and paper

Tearing

Reveal the core and texture of cardstock or paper by tearing it. Tearing towards you reveals the centre or 'core' of your paper. Tearing away from you produces a crisply torn edge.

Mix and match

1 Create a co-ordinating patterned paper border by cutting a contrasting strip of card slightly larger than the patterned paper. Apply glue.

2 Place the smaller strip of patterned paper in the centre of the contrasting strip. This will help draw the eye to the contrasting pattern and colour.

Crumpling

Add texture and a feeling of age to card and papers by crumpling them. Scrunch the sheet into a ball to produce a creased effect: the tighter the ball, the more textured the finished result will be.

Improvising papers

- *Use old sheet music as a background paper. Apply an archival spray first to make the papers safe to use in your scrapbook.*
- *Use a photograph enlarged to the size of your page as a background paper – a fantastic photo of a sunset or a winter scene makes for a great effect.*
- *Get some co-ordinating wallpaper samples from your local DIY store for a really unique page.*

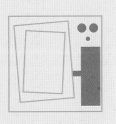

Sanding

Cardstock and paper with a contrasting-coloured core can be sanded to produce a softly worn effect. Using fine-grade sandpaper in a small circular motion produces the best results. Experiment with scrap before using a whole sheet.

Distressing

Create a shabby, weathered finish by distressing your card and paper. Combine tearing, crumpling and sanding, and then add colour by using an ink stamp (as above) or chalks or paints for a fabulous result.

1 ME & GRANDAD

Black card has been used to split the two co-ordinated patterned papers and make the photo jump off the page.

2 CARTE POSTALE

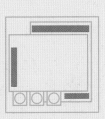

Black ink has been used to distress the card, adding movement and matching the theme and feel of the photo.

USING VELLUM

Vellum is a translucent paper available in a variety of colours, patterns and thicknesses. Its sheer quality can make attaching vellum difficult, so try using eyelets, brads, vellum glue or clips. Alternatively, hide the adhesive under embellishments or layers on the page. Vellum adds a soft, cloudy feel to your scrapbook pages, and is perfect for toning down strong colours or patterns.

Attaching layers of vellum

Use spiral clips to attach contrasting vellums, as most adhesive is visible through the translucent paper.

Materials

Vellum die cut motifs

Patterned and monotone vellum

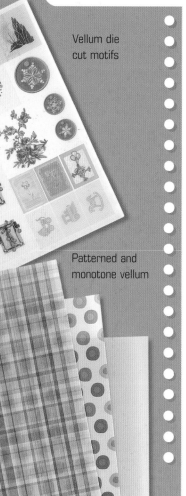

Journaling

Use your computer and print the characters on a sheet of vellum to create custom titles and journaling. Vellum is less porous than standard paper or card, and the ink takes a little while to dry. For a stunning effect, shake embossing powder onto the wet ink and then set it with a heat gun.

Die cuts

Use a die-cutting tool to create unique embellishments out of vellum with a soft and delicate look. Dies are available in hundreds of shapes and sizes.

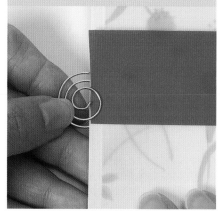

Embossing

Create beautiful, textured designs on vellum using a stencil and embossing stylus. The translucent quality of vellum means that there is no need for a light box. Simply place the sheet of vellum over the stencil and trace around the inside edge of the design with the embossing stylus. Turn the vellum over to reveal a raised, embossed image.

Using vellum as a window

1 Place a sheet of vellum over your photo and mark out with a pencil where you want to put your frame.

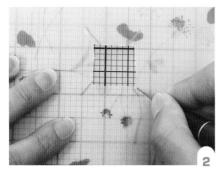

2 Using a craft knife, cut out a square. Cut small diagonal slits in each corner.

3 Fold and roll back the vellum to create your window.

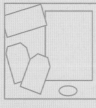

1 LASTING TIES

You can create your own vellum title with a font to match the theme of your page. Here, the title has been attached to a border made from co-ordinating patterned paper.

2 DELIGHT

Use matching coloured brads to attach your vellum. This avoids any glue marks that might show through the transparent paper.

"The Capacity

for Delight is

the Gift of

paying Attention"

Julia Cameron

STAMPING TECHNIQUES

Stamping allows you to introduce both designs and text into your scrapbook pages wherever you choose. Stamps are available either mounted onto wooden blocks or unmounted – choose unmounted to save both space and money.

Materials

Unmounted and mounted rubber stamps

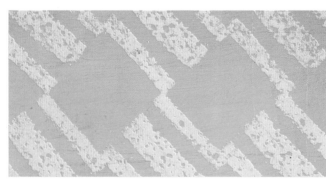

Using sponges as stamps

Medium-density sponges make good stamps. Choose a simple graphic shape for the stamp. Trace a design onto paper and cut it out. Attach the paper cut-out to the sponge and then cut around it.

Using metallic powder

Stamp on a fantasy finish with PVA glue and gold metallic powder.

Preparing mounted stamps

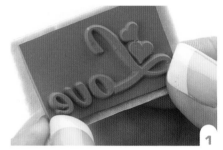

1 Remove the backing paper from the mounting foam to reveal the adhesive. Place the stamp on the sticky side and press down firmly.

2 Trim the excess rubber and mounting foam from around the image on the stamp. This will reduce the chance of ghost images being added to your work by the stamp edges.

3 The mounted stamp will cling to any smooth shiny object. An acrylic block makes the best, most stable surface for stamping.

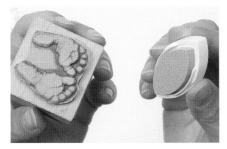

Loading ink

Ensure an even coverage of ink over the stamp, wiping away any excess with a wet-wipe or damp cotton swab.

tip *Try stamping with bleach onto a darker surface for an amazing effect.*

Letter stamping

There are a variety of wooden letter stamps available that will fit all themes. Create your own unique title or text in various fonts to suit.

1 THE EARTH LAUGHS

Clear acrylic squares have been stamped and coloured with alcohol inks. Additional gold and silver stamping helps to give this page a vintage feel.

2 LAUGHTER

Alphabet stamps with paint have been used for this title. Once dry, chalk was added to create a shadow in a co-ordinating colour.

USING DIE CUTS

Die cuts are fun features to use to embellish your pages. They can be purchased pre-cut and ready to use, or alternatively, you can make your own using die-cutting equipment, and any of the huge range of dies now available.

Embellished die cuts

Embellish your die cuts with chalks, inks, beads or glitter to co-ordinate them with your page's theme.

Materials

Die
Die-cutting tool

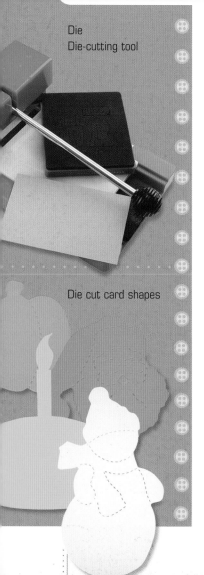

Die cut card shapes

1 Cut a piece of card or paper to size and place this over the design area on the die. Turn the die and paper over together and place them into the die-cutting tool.

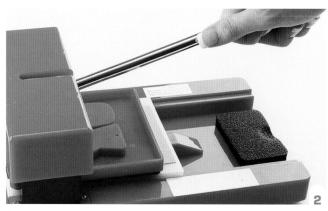

2 Slide the die and paper under the weight and press firmly to cut out the shape. Larger dies may need to be cut in two or three sections.

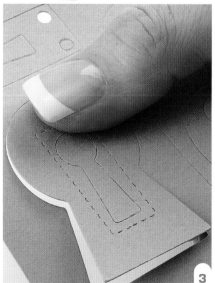

3 Remove the die from the cutter and gently press out the shape from the background paper or card.

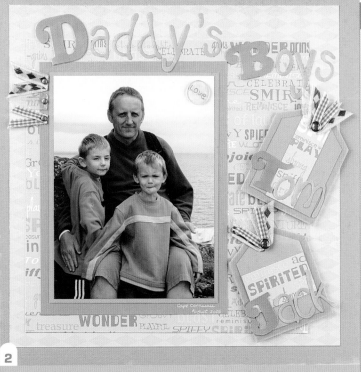

1 WATER BOY

Many suppliers produce co-ordinating die cuts to match their patterned papers. This scrapbooker has used several, alongside co-ordinating sticker letters.

2 DADDY'S BOYS

There are now several die-cutting systems that have a wealth of different fonts to choose from. Two different fonts are used here to emphasise the title and the boys' names.

3 ALWAYS

This scrapbooker has inked her die-cut letters with a metallic pen so that they co-ordinate with the copper theme that she has introduced with her embellishments.

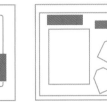

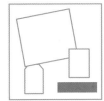

USING PUNCHES

Punches are among the staple equipment of any craft box and they are well worth the investment. From basic shapes to corner and border punches, there are a host of designs to choose from, and they all work well on scrapbook pages.

Materials

Punches

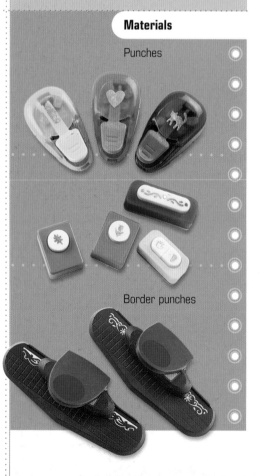

Border punches

Punching a border

1 Use a ruler and pencil to mark a point in the middle of the edge of your card or paper.

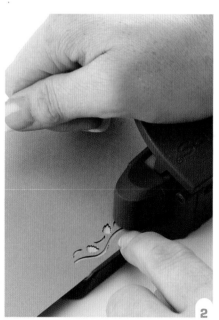

2 Align the punch with the pencil mark and press it down firmly to cut out the shape. Use the guidelines printed on the punch to move it along, and match the design against the first cut out before punching again.

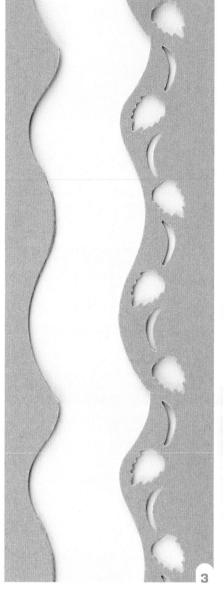

3 Work out in both directions from each side of the centre mark to complete the design and create a perfectly punched edge.

Creating different shapes

1 Using several different sizes of flower punch, you can punch different colours in each size.

2 Layer the flower to create a 3D embellishment. Finish this project by cutting a pot shape from brown cardstock.

1 MY WISH FOR YOU

Border punches can give a delicate touch to your projects. Here, all four edges of the patterned paper have been punched to complement the romantic theme.

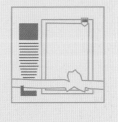

2 PHOEBE

You can use excess paper to punch out different shapes to use as embellishments. Here, flowers are mounted on top of each other to create a three-dimensional look.

WET EMBOSSING

Embossing creates the illusion of enamel work on scrapbook pages. It is the next step up from simple stamping and, with a little practice, can produce impressive results. The stamps are the same, but are combined with speciality ink pads and powders, and then set with a heat gun to form a glossy layer of colour.

Materials

Embossing pad

Embossing powder

Rubber stamp

Heat gun

2 Shake a generous amount of embossing powder over the wet stamped image, ensuring the whole image is covered. Pour the excess powder back into the jar.

1 Apply embossing ink to the surface of a rubber stamp before stamping an image firmly onto your card or paper.

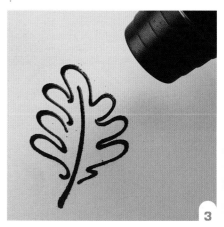

3 Gently heat the powdered image with a heat gun until it becomes glossy. Move the heat away once the powder has set.

Using an embossing pen

Use an embossing pen to outline a title or image and then apply embossing powder over the top.

Decorative embossing

Once perfected, the art of embossing can also be used to decorate frames for your photographs.

1 SEVEN

A subtle title has been created here with wet embossing by using clear embossing powder on black card. This ensures that the emphasis remains on the beautiful photograph.

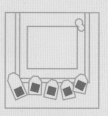

2 DREAM

Torn card makes a great surface to emboss on to. Here, the scrapbooker has individually torn around the letters to make her title and then embossed them, bringing the title to the forefront.

DRY EMBOSSING

Dry embossing allows you to add dimension to your pages by depressing an image into the surface of card or paper. Using a stencil and lightbox you can place images anywhere you choose.

Materials

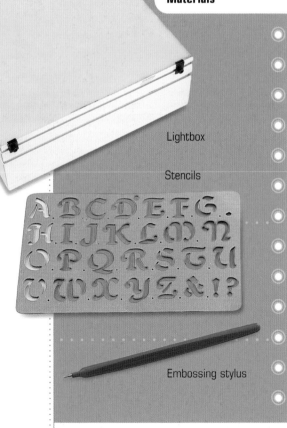

Lightbox

Stencils

Embossing stylus

Chalk embossing

1 Using a stencil, emboss into your chosen card.

2 Turn the card over. Use fine sandpaper to lightly sand the image.

Improvising a lightbox

If you don't have a lightbox, you can improvise with a sheet of glass or Lucite supported on bricks or books over a table lamp. Alternatively, you can tape your design and card to a sunny windowpane.

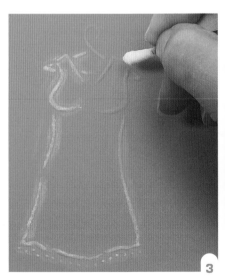

3 Use a cotton swab or chalk applicator to highlight the image, using white chalk to make the image pop out.

Using a stencil

1 Use a lightbox to illuminate a stencil, and highlight the areas to depress. Use lightweight card or paper to ensure that the design will be visible. Place a stencil upside down onto the lightbox. Use an embossing stylus to trace around the template.

2 Remove the stencil and lift the card from the lightbox to reveal the raised embossed image.

1 SUMMER

This scrapbooker has created a beautiful frame by using string underneath and de-embossing it. To make embossing stand out, use metallic rub-ons or gold spray ink.

2 A

Try using parchment craft (Pergamano) to create stunning pages. Use a graphic template to emboss first before using special Pergamano pens to trace the outline.

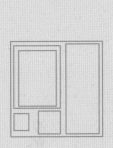

USING RUB-ONS

Rub-ons are available in a variety of images, designs and lettering. They are fast and simple for adding titles and journaling to your work. Rub-ons can be applied directly onto a number of surfaces, including photographs.

Materials

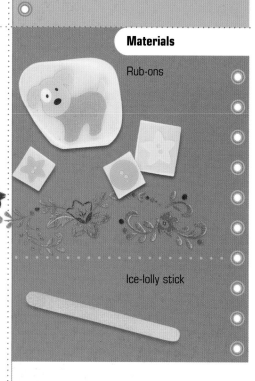

Rub-ons

Ice-lolly stick

1 Peel the backing from the rub-on and place the image onto your page.

2 Use an ice-lolly stick (or similar) to trace over the entire image gently. The image will become cloudy, indicating that it has separated from the top sheet.

Border rub-ons

Rub-ons are also available as borders, in a wide range of styles and sizes. They can add the perfect finishing touch to any theme or project.

3 Carefully peel back one corner or small area of the top sheet to check that the rub-on has adhered to the background. Replace the top sheet and rub over it again if the image has not transferred.

Select your image

For the best results, cut out your chosen image from the sheet before applying. This will avoid other images being transferred accidentally.

Positioning

Keep the backing paper in place until you are ready to apply the rub-on. Try out different positions until you are sure where to place the image.

1 PRETTY

Alphabet rub-ons come in various styles of fonts and can easily be used to complement a theme. This scrapbooker has mixed upper- and lowercase letters for a shabby, chic feel.

2 BROTHERS

The use of rub-ons has made the title look like it is printed straight onto the page, with the colours matching perfectly. The use of two different fonts together gives an eclectic look.

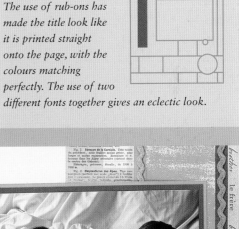

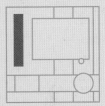

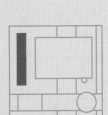

USING STICKERS

Every dedicated scrapbooker should have a supply of stickers. Whether they are colourful, patterned or plain and simple, you are sure to have a variety of stickers in your mound of supplies. Stickers are as easy to use as peel-and-stick, and they are among the most versatile scrapbooking products.

Using stickers as accents

Use matching coloured papers and stickers for a perfectly co-ordinated scrapbook page.

Materials

Padded stickers

Glitter stickers

Letter and number stickers

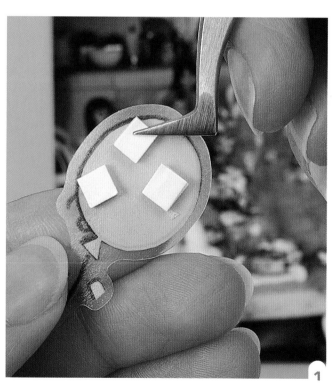

3D stickers

1 Place 3D foam pads evenly onto the back of the sticker, ensuring the pads are placed in the middle to avoid the centre collapsing.

2 Apply the sticker to your page for a fun, three-dimensional embellishment.

Making your own photo stickers

1 You can now use your computer to create your own photo stickers. Select the photographs to be printed as stickers (using photo manipulation software). Place a sheet of sticker paper into the printer and then print your images. Some manufacturers also offer photo-quality sticker paper for high quality results.

2 Just peel off the photo from the backing sheet and it is ready to use. Photo stickers come complete with adhesive and can be quickly and simply added to your design.

1 ALL THINGS GROW BETTER

There are now lots of cardstock stickers that match patterned papers for a perfectly co-ordinated page. Stickers come in various styles and themes – it's easy to find suitable stickers to match your scrapbook page.

2 IT'S THE LITTLE THINGS

Quotations and poems are available as stickers, and can be placed over any surface. Cardstock numbered stickers that match the patterned paper have also been used here.

smile big · love ya

all things grow better with

LOVE

laugh

friendship is blooming

HAPPY

2 0 0 3

it's the little things

Nature IS PAINTING FOR US, day after day, PICTURES OF INFINITE *beauty...*
John Ruskin

FRAMING

Frames highlight focal points on your scrapbook page. They are available in a huge range of shapes, sizes and styles – from ornately baroque to clean and simple. Adding a frame can make a small image much more significant, so try framing something you want to draw attention to.

Materials

Frames

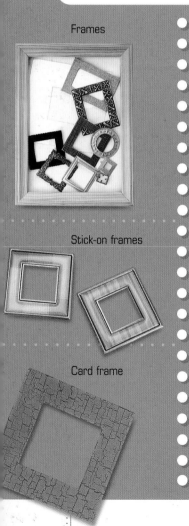

Stick-on frames

Card frame

Attaching with 3D tape
Use foam adhesive tape to attach a frame, and this will also add dimension to the frame.

Hanging on ribbon
'Hang' a frame on a length of ribbon to resemble a picture hung on a wall.

Applying glue dots
Textured frames can be tricky to attach as they often have an uneven surface underneath. Glue dots mould themselves to the contours of the frame and form a strong bond.

Framing elements

1 Place strong glue dots around the inside of the metal frame.

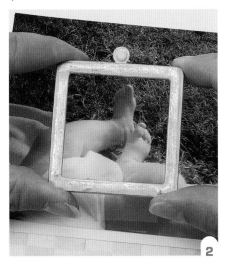

2 Choose the element in your photograph that you want to emphasise. Place the metal frame over the focal point to make this element pop out.

1 IT'S NOT DIRT

Try looking around your home for unique frames for your pages. This scrapbooker has used an old broken pocket watch to frame a close-up of her son's face after his first bike ride!

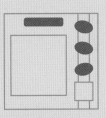

2 ALL YOU NEED IS...

Small metal frames are perfect for adding another photo to your scrapbook page. They also double up as a great embellishment.

its not dirt -its freedom!

All you need is . . . .

Love

Love

Love

I Love You

MAKING MOSAICS

You can mimic the style of Roman mosaics in minutes. Mosaic pages consist of photos cut into small squares and re-assembled like tiles on a floor. Mosaics can be used to stretch photos to fill more space on your page, as well as for artistic and eye-catching designs.

Materials

Craft knife

Ruler
(preferably metal)

Mosaic template

Cutting mat

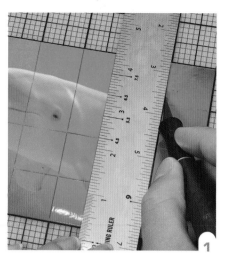

1 Place your photograph onto a mosaic cutting mat, using a small amount of repositional glue to keep it in place. Using a craft knife and metal ruler, follow the guidelines and cut the picture into evenly sized squares.

2 Transfer each photo square in turn to a mosaic template sheet, reconstructing the image in a grid format.

3 Use pieces of co-ordinating coloured card to separate images on a page.

Tips for mosaics

• *To begin with, experiment with photographs of subjects where it will not matter how you cut them up – flowers, gardens or buildings are ideal.*

• *When you progress to photographs of people, try not to cut through their faces, particularly not their eyes.*

• *You do not need to use the whole of every photograph. Move the image around the grid on the cutting mat until you have the pieces you want within the right squares.*

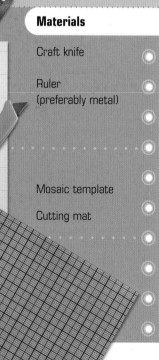

1 DISNEY DREAMS

This fabulous mosaic scrapbook page has been created mainly using postcards from Disney World. The scrapbooker has managed to incorporate five mosaic photos along with a title on this page.

2 CUTE

Mosaics can be any size – remember this if you are not comfortable cutting your photo into smaller pieces. This style of mosaic also works well for photos that have faces, as you do not need to cut into the face.

3 WISH

Mosaics don't have to be square – you can try using rectangle shapes as this scrapbooker has with co-ordinating patterned papers and repeat the shape with the photo. This is a great technique to make your photo look bigger on the page.

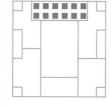

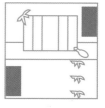

EYELETS

Few embellishments are as versatile as eyelets. An eyelet is a simple metal tube with a rolled collar at one end. The collar is set onto the visible side of your work. Eyelets can be used to hold layers of page together or purely for decorative effect. Look out for eyelets of different shapes, sizes and colours. Themed eyelets can also be fun additions to your work.

Materials

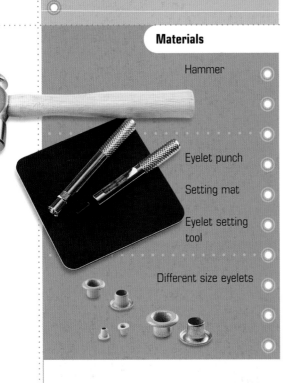

Hammer

Eyelet punch

Setting mat

Eyelet setting tool

Different size eyelets

1 Position the eyelet punch onto your card or paper on top of a setting mat. Hit the punch sharply with a hammer, giving one tap for each layer of card or paper you are punching through.

3 Insert the eyelet setting tool into the eyelet tube on the back of the paper. Tap the setter with a hammer three or four times.

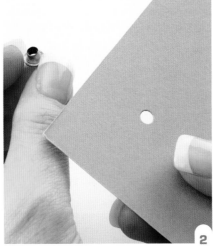

2 Pass an eyelet through the punched hole, so that the collar sits on the right side of the paper.

4 Once set, the closure should look like a flower. Turn the paper over to reveal the set eyelet on the right side of the work.

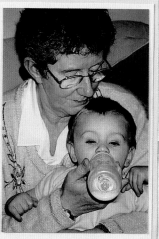

omfort

and

Cuddles

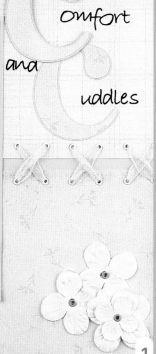

The joy

Dad

SUMMER

SUMMER

AUGUST

AUGUST

of a

BOY!
boy oh boy

SUMMER

2005

AUGUST

Will

1

2

3

BLUE EYES

Vincent

1 COMFORT AND CUDDLES

Use eyelets to create a pattern on your scrapbook page. Ribbon is used here to give the feel that the eyelets and ribbon are holding the patterned papers together like a patchwork.

2 THE JOY OF A BOY

Eyelets come in a variety of colours so it's easy to match them to your projects. Here, the sandy brown matches the cardstock and ties in with the theme of the photos.

3 BLUE EYES

Eyelets are also a great way to create mini books. Several mini books are used on this page – it's an easy way to incorporate lots of photos into your scrapbook.

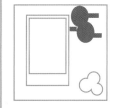

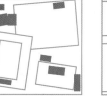

FASTENERS

Fasteners are a great way to attach papers and embellishments together without the aid of glue. Manufacturers now make fasteners in a variety of colours, shapes, sizes and themes. Check out your local office-supply stores for small and large paper fasteners as they can easily be altered with ink, embossing powders and paints.

Materials

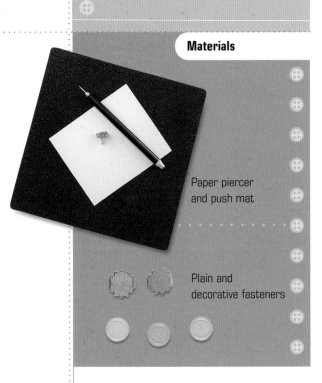

Paper piercer and push mat

Plain and decorative fasteners

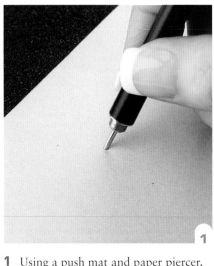

1 Using a push mat and paper piercer, create a hole where you want your fastener to go.

2 Remove your push mat and place your fastener into the hole you have created with the paper piercer.

3 Turn your paper over and separate the two prongs and fold them flat to the surface of the paper. Your fastener is now secure.

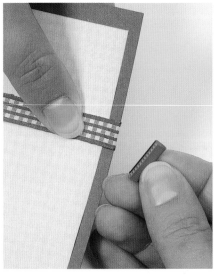

Using slide fasteners

This slide fastener can be used on the edge of a scrapbook page to hold ribbon and card in place. Once positioned, simply squeeze to secure.

Using tacks

1 Push your tack into your card or paper, ensuring you use a soft push mat underneath.

2 Using the flat edge of a small craft hammer, flatten the prongs to the page by gently bending.

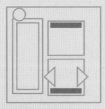

1 A LITTLE MIRACLE

Fasteners come in all shapes and colours. This scrapbooker has chosen brads with coloured crystal encased in them. Using brads is a great way to attach vellum, which can otherwise sometimes show glue marks.

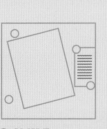

2 SMILE

The fasteners used here are hollow, which allows the use of co-ordinating stickers inside. They have been sealed using a dimensional adhesive, which gives a glossy finish to the fasteners.

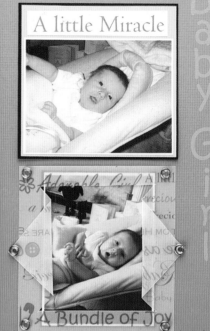

CHARMS

Charms are must-have embellishments that never seem to go out of fashion. They can add style, whimsy and meaning to your project – it depends on what you choose, and why. Threaded onto jump rings, charms can be hung from ribbon, fibres or chain. Add charms as you would jewellery accessories, and you will bring a little of your personality to the page.

Materials

Range of charms

Attaching charms with a jump ring

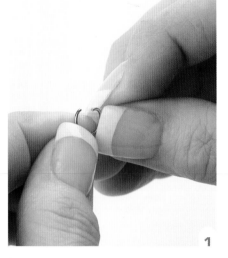

1

1 Hold the jump ring firmly on each side of its join – you may find it easier to use pliers for this. Twist the ring to open the join sideways, but do not pull the ring apart as this will distort its shape and make it difficult to close later.

2

2 Thread a charm onto the open jump ring before twisting the join closed. Thread the jump ring onto a length of fibre, chain or ribbon to hang the charm on your project.

Using double-sided sticky pads

If you want the charm to sit away from the surface of the card then invest in some double-sided sticky pads. They are clean, easy to apply, and some are extremely strong so the charm should not fall off.

Using a glue gun

Perhaps the simplest of all adhesive methods is glue. Your only real concern when using glue is that it is strong enough and will dry clear. There are many good glues on the market and a hot-glue gun is useful for this technique.

Themed embellishments

The right charm can add that special finishing touch to your page. Charms can be found to fit almost any theme, from birthdays and celebrations to moving to a new home.

Sewing

If the charm has a hole then you can use this to your advantage and sew the charm into position. If sewing directly onto the card, then pierce the card first with a pin to make it easier to attach. If backing onto a piece of fabric, sew the charm on first and stick the fabric into place.

1 PETER PAN

This page is full of hidden charms – look closely at the frame and you will see themed charms. The floral theme has been carried onto the paper with flower charms attached by brads.

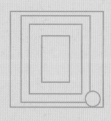

2 BEACH BOY

A unique themed border has been created using real seashells and sea charms sewn onto fabric, tied with ribbon and beads.

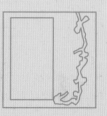

PLAQUES

Plaques come in all sorts of mediums, from metal and wood to clay and card. It's easy to make your own personal plaques using a number of techniques with the aid of a computer. Most plaques include a title, picture or quotation – and one can usually be found to suit any theme on your scrapbook page.

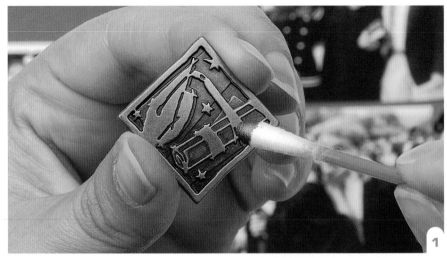

1 Using a metallic rub-on paint, you can easily change the colour of a plaque to match the colours on your scrapbook page.

Materials

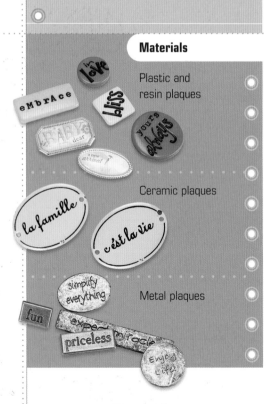

Plastic and resin plaques

Ceramic plaques

Metal plaques

2 Many plaques are self adhesive. Peel off the layer of paper to reveal the glue.

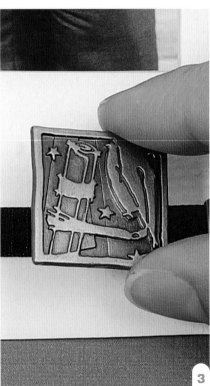

3 Attach to your page and press down firmly for the glue to hold.

Attaching plaques with fasteners

Fasteners are a great way to attach a plaque that has been pre-cut with a hole.

Using corner plaques

Metal corners look lovely on your scrapbook page or on your photos. Ensure you use a strong metal glue to adhere them.

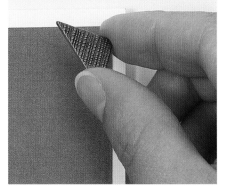

1 SCHOOL

This faux number plate looks very realistic. This type of ready-made plaque usually comes with an alphabet so you can choose your own title. Try re-creating your own using supplies ready at hand.

2 JACK

The plaque on this scrapbook page has been painted and then wiped so that the indented word is left with the paint, making the words on the plaque pop out.

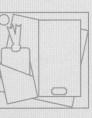

WIRE WORK

Wire is extremely easy to work with and it can be used delicately. There are different thicknesses, or gauges, of wire. Choose thinner, higher gauge wire to practise with, as it is easiest to manipulate. Try tracing the shape of words with wire to create titles or journaling, or thread a length of wire with beads and add it as an accent on a page.

Materials

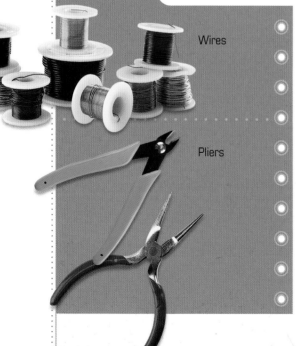

Wires

Pliers

Making a wire embellishment

1 For the example shown, 15cm (6 inches) of wire has been cut. Position round-nosed pliers on the wire just off centre and turn the wire back onto itself. Squeeze the two sides together.

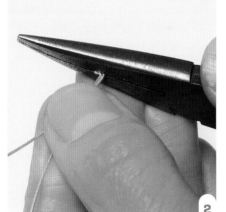

2 Hold firmly with flat-nosed pliers, and with the longer length of wire on the inside, gently start to form a coil.

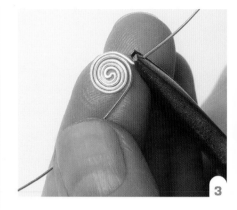

3 When you have reached the required size of coil, turn the outside length of wire to 90 degrees. Continue to wind the other length until it is opposite the first, then turn this to 90 degrees as well. The ends can be cut to about 6mm (¼ inch) to finish.

Attaching beads with wire

You can attach beads to wire and use them to embellish your page. After threading them on, pinch and twist the wire to prevent them from sliding off.

Twisting wire

1 Using wire cutters, cut a generous length of wire. Use the nose – or end – of long pliers to bend twists and spirals in the wire. Slide the spirals off the pliers as they are made before creating more twists in the length.

2 Distribute the twists and spirals along the wire to create an eclectic combination of loops and swirls. Trim off any excess wire before attaching the decoration across your page.

1 AS MOTHER OF THE BRIDE

This scrapbooker has incorporated an embellished wire headdress to both capture the big day and keep the memento safe.

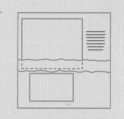

2 NOEL

The creator of this page has fashioned an eclectic wire border in gold to co-ordinate with the other gold embellishments and gold card and ribbon.

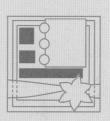

USING METAL SHEETS

Metal sheets are fun and versatile to use. They are perfect for adding an industrial or masculine feel to your pages, but can also be combined with other techniques to fit into almost any style or theme. Thin metal sheets can be die cut or trimmed with scissors into whatever shape you choose.

Stamping into metal sheets

1 Hold the die securely in position on the surface of the metal and firmly tap it on the top with a hammer. One hard tap with the hammer is better than a number of lighter ones as this gives a cleaner image.

Materials

Metal sheets

Hammer

Metal stamping die

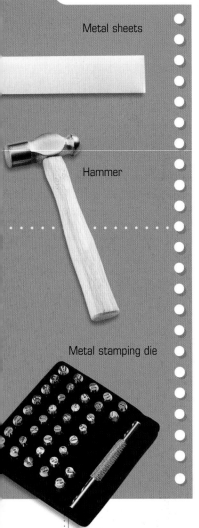

Using inks

For a mottled, weathered look, try stamping onto a metal sheet using alcohol inks.

Using rub-ons

You can apply rub-ons to metal sheets to create a more interesting embellishment.

Using patination fluids

If you want the look and feel of antique metal, try ageing the surface of a normal metal sheet with patination fluids.

2 The resulting image should be stamped cleanly into the surface of the metal. Other stamped images can be added for decorative effects, words or phrases. Highlight the stamped areas by painting over them with acrylic paint and wiping away the excess to leave the stamped areas filled with colour.

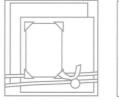

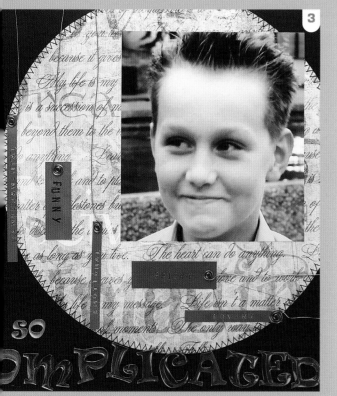

1 CHERISH

Metal can come in various forms of embellishments. Here, metal photo corners emphasise the photo's prominence on the page.

2 FALL

The colour of the stamped metal has been changed by holding it over a flame to create this beautiful patinated effect. Copper metal letters have also been used for the themed title.

3 OH SO COMPLICATED

Strips of metal have been embossed here using a label maker. The metal has been stamped into using a stamp die set and stamped onto using solvent-based ink. The metal strips are complemented by the copper lettering of the title.

USING BUTTONS

Everyone has a box of buttons just waiting to be used and now is the time to go raid it. Buttons come in all shapes, sizes and colours, and are also wonderfully tactile. Buttons can be used in many ways for depth and design – and they do not necessarily involve stitching.

Stitching a button on paper

Place a foam mat under your work. Position the button on your project and use a large needle or paper piercer to mark the page through the holes in the button. Start stitching from the reverse side and secure the ends of your thread with acid-free tape or adhesive tabs.

Glue dots on flat-backed buttons

Attach a glue dot to the reverse of a flat-backed button and then simply press the button onto the page.

Novelty buttons

Fun novelty buttons can be found in a vast range of shapes and colours. They make great embellishments for all kinds of themes. Build up an inspiring collection that will help you to always add that perfect finishing touch to your pages.

Materials

Buttons of varying sizes, shapes and colours

Creating a sewn-on effect

Thread embroidery floss or fibre through the holes in the button and tie it on the front for a fake sewn-on effect. Then attach the button with a glue dot.

1

2

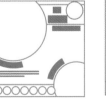

3

1 MOMENTS IN TIME

This scrapbooker has replicated the buttons from the patterned paper to tie in with the theme of this beautiful heritage page.

2 PHOEBE

Co-ordinating coloured buttons are used here to match the circles on the patterned paper.

3 KATE

This page was created using digital scrapbooking software. This allows you to add embellishments just as you would with a conventional page. Here, the buttons in the corner of the page complement the heritage theme.

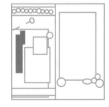

USING RIBBONS

Ribbons are a safe and decorative way to embellish your scrapbook pages. Even the shortest length of ribbon can be used to add a soft and feminine look to scrapbook designs. Tie ribbon across the page for a fast and simple border, tie bows, weave ribbons through frames, or use them to hang charms and other embellishments.

Materials

Ribbons

Scissors

Using ribbons as embellishments

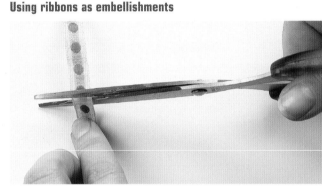

1 Cut equal lengths of co-ordinating ribbons.

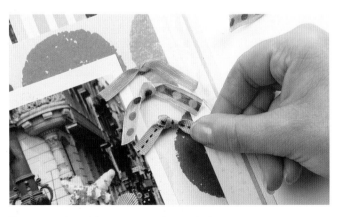

2 Tie them in loose knots and attach them to your page using glue dots.

Making ribbon roses

1 Snip off the top of the eye of the needle. Place a very small blob of glue on the cut end of the ribbon and then place it in the eye of the needle.

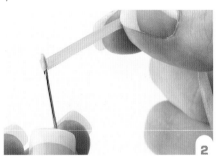

2 Twist the ribbon around the needle several times to form the bud of the rose.

3 To make petals, twist the ribbon into a loop. Dot tacky glue to the underside of the rose and secure the twist to it. Repeat this step five to six times to build up the layers of petals.

Attaching with ribbons

You can use ribbons to attach other embellishments, such as tags, to your layout.

Matching ribbons to the theme

Here, a soft pink wide organza ribbon makes for a sweet decorative element that complements the pink bow theme of the photograph.

1 TIMELESS

This patterned paper looks so realistic with the lace and fibres printed on it. The scrapbooker has cleverly sewn and glued real ribbon and fibres over the top to give a genuine three-dimensional look.

2 FIRST KISS

Choose ribbons that match the colours of your background and accentuate your photo by creating a border of ribbons. Make evenly spaced holes around the border, thread your ribbon through, and tie in a bow.

FIBRES & THREADS

Use fibres and threads to add texture – try soft fluffy mohair or funky, chunky yarns. There is plenty of choice. Capture the feeling of your favourite sweater by adding fibres from it to a scrapbook page.

Materials

Decorative fibres and threads

Stitching

You can stitch with decorative fibres. Start and finish on the right side of your work, and tie the ends as part of the design.

Attaching tags

Thread assorted fibres through a tag to add texture and colour.

Embellishing borders

Wrap fibres and threads around borders to link them with features on the page.

Using with eyelets

Thread fibres through pairs of eyelets and tie them on the front of your work in a simple knot or bow.

Embellishing with fibre

1 To embellish this wooden letter, distress it with sandpaper and tie fibre around it.

2 Add glue to the back of the letter and place it down in a single aperture frame.

How to use fibres and threads

• *If stitching onto cardstock, first pierce holes in it using a piercing or pricking tool. This will enable the thread to slip through the hole quickly and easily.*

• *Try not to use too long a length of thread. This will avoid knots and tangles and accidental tearing of your cardstock.*

• *Try using several different threads with a variety of textures on one page layout.*

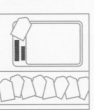

1 THE COLOUR OF SUMMER

Various colours of fibre are introduced here to reflect the changing sunflower colours. A variety of fibres and threads have been threaded through the tops of tags to add colour and texture.

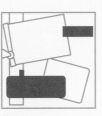

2 BOYISH CHARM

Fibres matching the colours of the page are wrapped around the side of the photo, fixed by attaching a coin charm. Fibre can also be used as a decorative closure as demonstrated on the file folder.

USING FABRIC

Fabric can be used in much the same way as paper in a design. Fabrics offer scrapbookers opportunities for working with texture. Textiles can be stitched or used together with other techniques to emphasise their qualities.

Materials

Fabrics in a range of colours and textures

Creating a layered fabric border

1 Use a craft knife or scissors to hand-cut around the flowers in daisy lace netting to make a border.

2 Adhere the cut lace border along the edge of your paper.

3 Place a ribbon along the top of the border, to conceal the rough edges.

Patchwork

Make a patchwork using scraps of fabric. Stick the fabric to a sheet of cardstock and then stitch over the joins in the fabric.

Creating stencilled fabric

This fabric letter has been created by placing a letter stencil over a piece of fabric.

Printing journaling on fabric

Choose a light-coloured fabric. Attach the fabric to paper using a repositionable adhesive and then run it through the printer.

Mounting photos on fabric

Give your photographs a lift by mounting them onto co-ordinated fabric to match your page.

1 CHANTILLY LACE

The soft lace border with its muted colour matches the bride's dress beautifully. The page has been finished off with a glittery fabric butterfly.

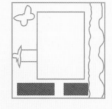

2 COMFORT

Use up scraps of fabric by incorporating them onto your pages. Scraps are used here to join the frame together, with little woven off-cuts embellishing the border.

STITCHING TECHNIQUES

You can attach layers by stitching them together rather than using adhesive. Stitching is also a simple technique for decorating a page. Use different stitches and colours to complement the theme and style of your photographs.

Materials

Threads
Tape measure

Scissors

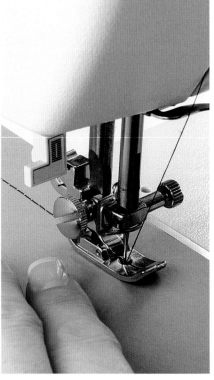

Stitching with a sewing machine

For fast, professional results, use a sewing machine. A regular sewing machine can stitch through many layers of cardstock and paper.

Handstitching

Use handstitching for a homely, rustic look. Start on the reverse of your project, securing the end of the thread with acid-free adhesive tape or an adhesive tab.

Using stitching templates

Stitching templates can be used for evenly spaced handstitching. Place your project on a push mat and use a paper piercer to mark each stitching hole.

Fake stitching

If sewing is not your thing, make fake stitching using an archival pen. Almost any stitch can be drawn.

CheRish

PURE (pyoor) 1. free from anything that taints 2. simple 3. innocence

ENDURING (en-door-ing) 1. lasting; permanent 2. continuing on until the end

LEGACY (leg-'e-se) 1. something passed through a family, handed down as from an ancestor

CHERISH (cher-ish) 1. to hold dear 2. to treasure, adore, value and love

MEMORIES (mem-'e-rez) 1. the power to recall sensory experiences from the past 2. the act of remembering

FOREVER (for-ev-'er) 1. for always, without end 2. without the bonds of time; eternal

TRADITION (tre-dish-'en) 1. passing down of beliefs and customs from one generation to the next 2. long-accepted and reoccurring practices associated with specific occasions

AARAN

w and forever

1

believe there are no limits but the sky.....

2

3

NEVER QUIT BUILT TOUGH

CANCER IAN

FEEL

aRan

1 CHERISH

Create a patchwork-style look by layering different patterned papers and then using your sewing machine to stitch them all together.

2 BELIEVE

The design of the bridge in the photograph has inspired the diamond effect background. The shapes have been cut from fabric and then overstitched on a sewing machine.

3 AARAN

Sewing machines have various different styles of stitching. A double stitch has been incorporated here using a black-and-white thread in keeping with the colour and feel of the page.

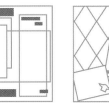

BEADING

A touch of beading can bring glamour to clothes and the same is true of scrapbook projects. Eye-catching beads can add sparkle and colour; they can be bold and dramatic, or tiny and delicate. Make the most of the many styles and sizes of beads that are available.

Materials

Range of beads

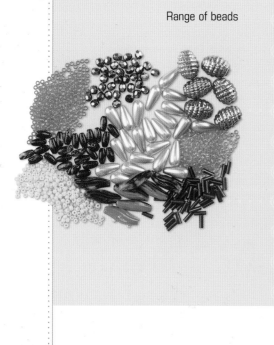

Using patterns

Beads can be added quickly and easily by sticking them onto an embellishment. Apply in a pattern or design, as here.

Using jewellery

Recycle beaded hair ornaments and thrift store jewellery.

Beadlings

Beadlings are fun to make with a few beads and some fine wire. Patterns are readily available and you can create beautiful, intricate items.

Making a beaded 3-D letter

1 Cut inside the outline of the letter with a craft knife. Then cut around the text box, and cut more card to the same size.

2 Mount the negative of your letter onto a second piece of card, using foam dots for a 3-D effect. Remove the pad coverings with a craft knife.

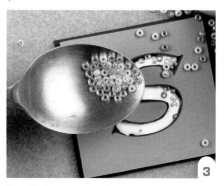

3 Fill the aperture between your cards pieces with glue. Pour in seed beads, fill in any gaps and press down evenly.

Stitching beads onto paper

Papers with pre-stitched embroidery are perfect for adding beaded embellishments because the holes have already been made.

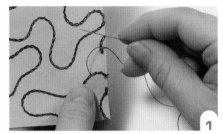

1 Gather together beads, a needle and thread in a complementary colour. Thread the needle and bring it up through the back of the paper, using one of the holes.

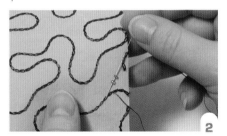

2 Decide how many beads can fit into the space between the holes. Thread on the beads and take the needle down through the next hole along.

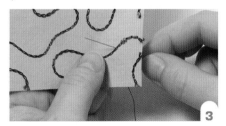

3 Bring the needle up through the next hole, ready to add on the next beads.

1 SUMMER GARDEN

. . . .

Create little beadlings to add a unique theme to your scrapbook page. The delicate butterfly beadlings on this page co-ordinate with the patterned paper and garden theme of the page.

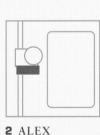

2 ALEX

. . . .

This scrapbooker has made a beautiful beaded frame and floral embellishment to match the patterned paper she has used. Although each bead here was stitched in place, you can achieve the same effect with adhesive.

SHRINK PLASTIC

Shrink plastic is a versatile and fun material. Choose from clear, frosted, white or black sheets. They can be coloured with ink, pencils or chalk before shrinking with a heat gun or in the oven. Shrink plastic reduces to one-third of its original size when heated.

3 Colour in the design using pencils, inks or crayons.

Materials

Shrink plastic sheets

Heat gun

1 Score the shrink plastic sheet lightly with sandpaper.

2 Stamp the design onto the plastic using either fabric ink or a permanent ink.

4 Carefully cut out the design. If required, a hole will need to be punched in the plastic at this stage.

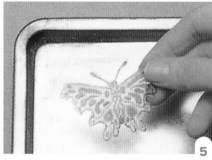

5 To shrink the plastic, place the piece onto a baking tray and heat in an oven at 140ºC / 275ºF for 3–5 minutes – or use a heat gun or hair-dryer.

Die cuts
Shrink plastic can be die cut to create glass-like embellishments.

Applying rub-ons
Apply rub-ons to shrink plastic. When the plastic is exposed to heat, the rub-ons will also shrink.

1 BE WHO YOU ARE

A large title has been created here, before placing it in the oven to shrink. This large title gives emphasis to the journaling.

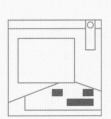

2 I SEE ART AND BEAUTY

This poetic title was created by shrinking die-cut words and mixing them with printed words directly onto cardstock.

INQUISITIVE

THOUGHTFUL

INQUIRING

U aRE

While the other children were watching the events of sports day, you were enthralled by the ants in the grass. I managed to zoom in with my camera from the other side of the field to capture this moment. I want to encourage you to continue to be who you are, notice things and ask questions – it's the only way to learn and grow.
July 2005

I see Art and Beauty in your face

GRANDMA

USING CLAY

Roll or mould clay into unusual features to add a special touch to your pages. Air-dry or oven-bake types of clay are available in a number of colours. Stamp out journaling, create fake stones and gems, and colour the clay with chalks, inks, paints or by applying metallic rub-ons.

Materials

Air-dry or
oven-bake clay

Rolling pin
Push-out or flexible
moulds
Biscuit cutters
Rubber stamps

Creating gradated clay sheets

1 Roll out a sheet of pink clay and another of blue. Cut a triangle of each colour and place them together on your work surface to form a rectangular sheet. Fold the sheet in half.

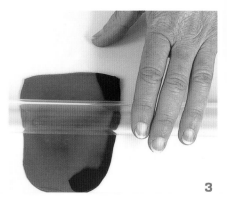

3 Fold the sheet in half again, in the same way, and roll out lengthways. Continue folding in half and rolling, keeping the edges neat. You will find that the colours begin to blend in the central area.

2 Roll out the sheet lengthways, or pass it through a pasta machine. The blue side of the clay is clearly visible opposite the pink side with a mixture of the colours appearing between.

4 After about 30 rollings, the clay will form a sheet that grades from pink through violet to blue. The clay can now be used to form embellishments for your pages.

Cutting out shapes

Use a biscuit cutter or similar to cut out shapes from rolled-out clay.

Using moulds

Use a push-out or flexible mould to shape ornate items quickly. Simply press the clay into the mould to form the shape, remove it with care and dry.

Using rubber stamps

Roll out clay to about an inch thick and use a rubber stamp to imprint shapes.

1 ME

The base of a small cat's-eye ink-pad has been used here to cut the petals that make this dimensional flower embellishment. Give some shine to your project by coating the dried clay with a glossy sealant.

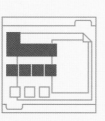

2 FLOWER GIRL

Use alphabet stamps to push a title into clay. Metal flower embellishments have also been pushed into clay to reinforce the flower theme.

all the pieces of me that make up my world!

GLITTER & SAND

Glitter and sand can add dimension, texture and – in the case of glitter – a touch of sparkle to your projects. For movement, make a shaker box or – if you are feeling adventurous – make a shaker title. For classic memorabilia, grab a handful of sand from the beach when you are next on holiday.

2 Pour glitter or sand into the centre of the aperture. Slowly peel away the backing of the double-sided tape and place the second square evenly on top to seal.

Materials

Glue pen

Glitter or sand

Making a shaker box

1 Cut two 9x9cm (3½x3½ inch) squares from a strip of card. Using a large square punch, punch an aperture square in the centre of one of the squares. Cover the front of the punched square aperture with a piece of transparency and turn over. Using double-sided tape, create a sealed border around the outside of the aperture.

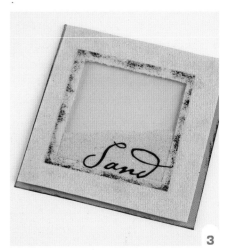

3 Turn the shaker box over and using a wet glue, glue all around the square border. Sprinkle sand over the glue ensuring an even coverage. Carefully shake off the excess.

Embellishing with glitter or sand

1 Use a wet glue pen to write your title – or start by following a template if you prefer even lettering.

2 Sprinkle glitter or sand generously over the glue, ensuring it is evenly covered.

3 Shake the excess off onto paper and tip it back into its pot. Set your project aside to dry. When the adhesive has dried, use a fine brush to remove loose glitter or sand from around the edges of the image.

1 OCEANSIDE

Bring a real feel of the beach to your holiday pages by adding sand. It is easily adhered with wet glue – just shake the sand on, leave to dry and then shake the excess off.

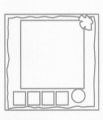

2 NOEL

Use a glitter pen to trace over lettering. It really enhances that Christmas feeling. Finish your scrapbook page off by glittering any torn edges to give them a sparkle too.

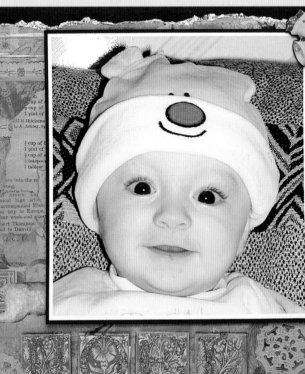

USING CHALKS

Use chalks in the same way as your make-up. Go for single colours, or blend shades and tones for drama. The latest chalks include shimmer finish in a wide variety of colours for a subtle touch of sparkle.

Materials

Chalk set and applicator

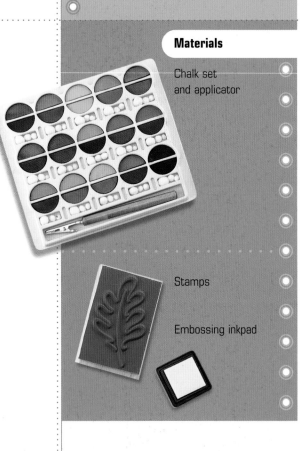

Stamps

Embossing inkpad

Creating a chalked image

1 Use a water-based inkpad with your stamp. Have the stamp facing you and ensure that you cover it evenly with ink.

2 Stamp the image onto the card. Using a small applicator, gently dab chalk onto the image. Work under a bright light to see the clear image.

3 When the image is covered with a layer of chalk, use a white eraser to neaten the edges.

Tips for using chalks

• *Create your own unique backgrounds by blending together different colours and shades. Try blending with different materials, such as cotton balls or sponges, for a variety of interesting effects.*

• *Highlight or shade lettering and die cuts to really make them stand out.*

• *Always have an eraser to hand, in case of mistakes.*

• *Apply a spray fixative when you have finished to ensure that your chalked work doesn't get smudged.*

GROOVY CHICK!

GROOVY BABY

DIG IT !!

EDEN
25-05-2002
CLIVE'S 46TH BIRTHDAY PARTY
"60'S"

LOVE
that
face

That cheeky, chubby face – where have I seen that before?
The beaming smile that goes all the way up to the eyes looks kind of familiar.
A confident wave for the camera, happy in my own skin. That's something else I recognise.

All of these traits I can now see in the face of Jack at the same age. Its wonderful really, when this photo was taken all this was yet to come and in the meantime here I am, Simply Me.

1 LOVE THAT FACE

This scrapbooker has used chalks to tone down the whiteness of the background to tie in with the black, white and grey theme of her scrapbook page.

2 GROOVY CHICK

You can create your own patterned paper by using dampened chalk. This scrapbooker has used this technique to match the background colours to the photograph.

3 SIMPLY ME

Give a weathered look to your titles by chalking around the edge. This scrapbooker has chosen not to paint her chipboard letters but to give them some emphasis by chalking them.

USING PAINT

Watercolour and acrylic paints have found a new outlet in scrapbooking. Use them for colour washes on backgrounds, combine them with resist techniques or add a texture medium for three-dimensional colour.

Materials

Watercolour or acrylic paints

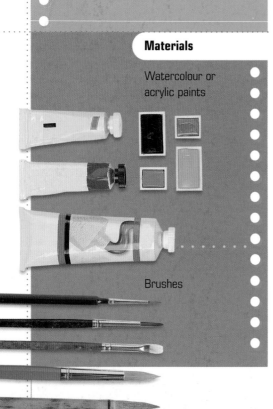

Brushes

Applying paint with stamps

1 Load acrylic paint onto a foam brush and carefully paint the raised area of the stamp, making sure it is evenly covered. Clean away any excess using a wet-wipe. Stamp the image lightly onto the card, taking care not to twist the stamp.

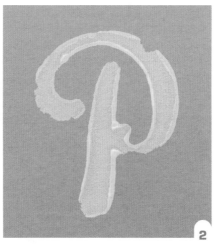

2 Allow the paint to dry completely. Then enhance the image using a fine paintbrush, and add dimension by shading with chalks.

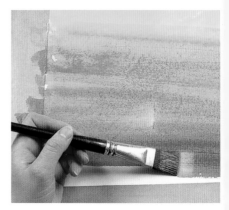

Creating gradated backgrounds

Mix three colours of paint that will blend well together – for example, red, orange and yellow. Paint one third of the paper with the yellow. Paint the next third orange, starting by overlapping the two colours. Use a damp brush to conceal the seam. Paint the remainder of the paper red, once again using a damp brush to blend the colours.

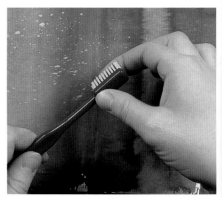

Spattering backgrounds

Dip an old toothbrush in some paint. Pointing it away from you, hold it over the paper and use your forefinger to spatter paint. Repeat this with other colours to create a multicoloured effect.

TO ACCOMPLISH **GREAT THINGS** WE MUST DREAM AS WELL AS ACT. —ANATOLE FRANCE

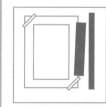

This is Lily, EllaMae's oldest friend and the daughter of my best friend Angelika. Lily has been part of our lives for nearly five years now, and although the girls are now separated by five and a half thousand miles they are still great friends.

Lily is a sweet, kind little girl, who is as cheeky and stubborn as EllaMae... Geli and I have seen some really funny stand-offs between them over the past few years!!

I believe their friendship is true and will last, and I love watching Lily grow into the bright, beautiful young girl she is becoming...

1 WANTED

If your cardstock is too dark you can use a cream paint to lighten it. Foam stamps have been used here for the title, and the edges have been chalked to create a shadow.

2 GREAT THINGS

A few simple brushes of paint is all it needs to make a title pop out of your page. A darker brown paint was used here for the background on top of the beige base card.

3 TOTALLY LILY

For a really striking title, use a contrasting background colour. Here, white on green and blue and different fonts have been used to make the title pop out.

USING INKS

Inks can bring a graphic touch to a scrapbook page. Fluid inks can be dripped onto the page and there are a variety of inkpad types available – chalk, pigment, solvent-based and dye – each for a specific purpose. Experiment and combine techniques for wonderful effects.

Materials

Inks

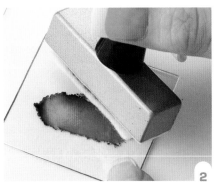

Creating an inked embellishment

1 Apply three to four drops of coloured alcohol ink onto a felt applicator.

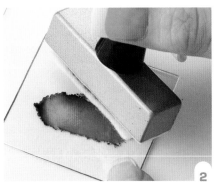

2 Lightly dab the applicator onto the surface of a clear overlay square, turning it to mix the colours.

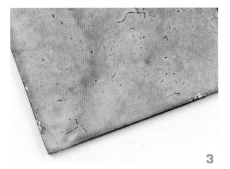

3 Blow onto the wet ink to blend the colours together for an overlay with a soft, muted effect. This technique works well on a non-porous surface.

Achieving a marbled background

1 Fill a tray with water. Slowly drop ink into the water, using as many different colours as you like. Mix the inks around the surface of the water.

2 Place a sheet of paper carefully on the water's surface. Leave it in place until you see the ink coming through.

3 Carefully lift the paper up. Hold it above the water to let the surplus run off. Place it on newspaper to dry.

1 MOST WANTED

The vintage feel of this lovely leathered surface has been achieved by crumpling card and then spraying it with walnut ink several times.

2 PEACOCK BUTTERFLY

Create a weathered effect by inking the edges of your card and papers. Contrasting and co-ordinating colours have been used on all the edges of this layout.

3 JACK & ANGEL

Alcohol ink has been used on a clear overlay to give it a mottled look. By using several co-ordinating colours you can easily match them to your chosen patterned papers.

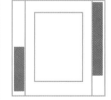

RESOURCES

All of the products used in this book should be readily available from your nearest arts and crafts shop. However, it is also worth exploring the many scrapbooking websites on the Internet, to discover new products or track down more elusive items.

LOCAL ARTS AND CRAFTS SHOPS

UK

Hobbycraft
www.hobbycraft.co.uk
Tel: 0800 027 2387

Creative Crafts
www.creativecrafts.co.uk
Tel: 01962 856266

Scrapaholic
www.scrapaholic.co.uk
Tel: 01474 702553

Smithcraft
www.smitcraft.com
Tel: 01252 342626

Total Papercrafts
www.totalpapercrafts.co.uk
Tel: 01474 832814

Australia

Eckersley's Arts, Crafts and Imaginations
www.eckersleys.com.au
Tel: 1300 657 766

North America

Ben Franklin Crafts & Frames
www.benfranklinstores.com
Tel: 262 681 7000

Hobby Lobby
www.hobbylobby.com
Tel: 405 745 1100

Michaels
www.michaels.com
Tel: 800.MICHAELS

WEBSITES

Many of these websites either allow you to order directly (and ship internationally) or list shops where their products are available.

3M
www.3M.com
Adhesives, including glue sticks, specialty tapes, foam tape squares and spray adhesives; also transparencies and laminating supplies

7 Gypsies
www.7gypsies.com
Scrapbooking supplies, including unusual embellishments

Above the Mark
www.abovethemark.com
Quality unmounted rubber stamp dies

Anima Designs
www.animadesigns.com
Unique art stamps, findings, ephemera. Journals, found object jewellery, consignment gallery, journaling supplies and more

Anna Griffin, Inc.
www.annagriffin.com
Fine decorative papers and embellishments for scrapbooking and paper arts

Ariden Creations
www.aridencreations.com
Wood embellishments for scrapbook pages

Art Impressions
www.artimpressions.com
Original rubber stamps

Autumn Leaves
www.autumnleaves.com
Scrapbooking paper, books and
embellishments

Bazzill
www.bazillbasics.com
Cardstock

Canson
www.canson.com
Archival photo organisation, including
photo corners, albums and papers

Carolee's Creations
www.caroleescreations.com
Scrapbooking paper and embellishments

Clearsnap
www.clearsnap.com
Ink and rubber stamp manufacturer,
including stamp wheels

Cloud 9
www.cloud9design.biz
Makers of Halo eyelet stamps

Colorbok
www.colorbok.com
Scrapbooking albums, paper and
embellishments

Craf-T
www.craf-tproducts.com
Rainbow chalks for embellishments

Crafters Pick
www.crafterspick.com
Makers of Ultimate glue

Crafts, etc.
www.craftsetc.com
Decorative and unique papers

Creative Imagination
www.cigift.com
Papers, supplies and embellishments

Delta
www.deltacrafts.com
Acrylic paints and craft supplies

Deluxe Designs
www.deluxecuts.com
Scrapbook papers, supplies and
embellishments

Design Originals
www.d-originals.com
Scrapbook papers, supplies and
embellishments

DiBona Designs
www.dibonadesigns.com
Fine art stamps

DMD
www.dmdind.com
Paper and craft supplies

Dreamweaver Stencils
www.dreamweaverstencils.com
Brass templates and embossing supplies

Dymo
www.dymo.com
Label makers and supplies

EK Success
www.eksuccess.com
Scrapbook papers, supplies and
embellishments

Family Treasures
www.familytreasures.com
Paper punches

Fancifuls, Inc.
www.fancifulsinc.com
Brass charms and embellishments

Foofala
www.foofala.com
Scrapbook and paper art embellishments

Frederix
www.fredrixartistcanvas.com
Artist canvas

Glue Dots International
www.gluedotsinternational.com
Adhesive dots for papercraft
applications

Golden
www.goldenpaints.com
Quality line of paints, fluid acrylics and
mediums for art

Hero Arts
www.heroarts.com
Art stamps

Hot Potatoes

www.hotpotatoes.com

Art stamps

Impress Rubber Stamps

www.impressrubberstamps.com

Rubber stamps

Jacquard

www.jacquardproducts.com

Artist paints and pearlescent powders

Jewelcraft

www.jewelcraft.biz

Embellishments, including unique nailhead designs

Judikins

www.judikins.com

Stamps and supplies, including Diamond Glaze

Just for Fun

www.jffstamps.com

Fine art stamps and supplies

K and Co.

www.kandcompany.com

Scrapbook paper, albums and embellishments

KI Memories

www.kimemories.com

Scrapbook paper, supplies and embellishments

Lasting Impressions

www.lastingimpressions.com

Brass templates and embossing supplies

Liquitex

www.liquitex.com

Paint and craft finishes

Ma Vinci's Reliquary

www.crafts.dm.net/mall/reliquary

Unmounted art stamps

Magic Scraps

www.magicscraps.com

Scrapbook embellishments and supplies

Making Memories

www.makingmemories.com

Scrapbook paper, tools, supplies and embellishments

Marvy Uchida

www.uchida.com

Markers and ink for papercrafting

Me and My Big Ideas

www.meandmybigideas.com

Scrapbook paper, supplies and embellishments

Midori

www.midoriribbon.com

Ribbon, including printed varieties

Paper Parachute

www.paperparachute.com

Paper for paper art and scrapbooking

Paper Source

www.paper-source.com

Paper for paper art and scrapbooking

Papers by Catherine

www.papersbycatherine.com

Paper for paper art and scrapbooking

Pixie Press

www.pixiepress.com

Scrapbook papers and supplies

Plaid

www.plaidenterprises.com

Craft supplies including stamps, papers and tools

Pressed Petals

www.pressedpetals.com

Pressed flowers for embellishments

Prism

www.prismpapers.com

Large selection of fine cardstock for papercrafting, including exclusive textured line

Provocraft

www.provocraft.com

Coluzzle plastic template system

Prym-Dritz

www.prymdritz.com

Sewing notions and supplies

PSX

www.psxdesign.com

Art stamps and supplies

Purple Onion Designs
www.purpleoniondesigns.com
Art stamps and supplies

Quickutz
www.quickutz.com
Die-cut machine, unique alphabet and shapes dies

Ranger
www.rangerink.com
Rubber stamp and paper art inks and supplies

ReadySet
www.readysettools.com
Unique eyelet setting tool

River City Rubber Works
www.rivercityrubberworks.com
Art stamps with a humorous side and other unusual supplies

Rollabind
www.rollabind.com
Binding machines and supplies

Scrapworks
www.scrapworks.com
Scrapbook papers, tolls, supplies and embellishments

Sizzix
www.sizzix.com
Personal die-cutting machine

Stampington and Co.
www.stampington.com
Fine art and paper art supplies and books

Thermo Web
www.thermoweb.com
Adhesive

Tsukineko
www.tsukineko.com
Ink for rubber stamping and paper art

Tumblebeasts
www.tumblebeasts.com
Scrapbook stickers including unique textured stickers

Uhu
www.uhu.de
Glue sticks and adhesives

US Shell
www.usshell.com
Shells and sea horses for craft and paper projects

Victorian Trading Co,
www.victoriantradingco.com
Victorian goods for the home and crafter

The Vintage Workshop
www.thevintageworkshop.com
Vintage clip art and printable surfaces for fabric and paper arts

Walnut Hollow
www.walnuthollow.com
Wood embellishments and wood and paper burning tools for scrapbook and paper arts

Westrim
www.westrimcrafts.com
Scrapbook and paper art embellishments

Wordsworth
www.wordsworthstamps.com
Paper, stamps and stencils for paper arts and scrapbooking

Wrights
www.wrights.com
Sewing trims

X-Acto
www.hunt-corp.com
X-Acto knives and blades

INDEX

CREDITS

Quarto would like to thank the following for allowing images to be reproduced:

Key: t = top, b = bottom, l = left, r = right

Photographs:
Steve Bavister 9t, 9b, 14l, 14c, 34, 36tr, 37l
Paul Ridsdale 35bl, 35br

Scrapbook pages and projects:
Meryl Bartho 45, 66b, 74, 131b
Amila Boteju 76
Helen Campling 80l, 83b, 87b, 99b, 107t, 113b, 121b, 129tr, 131tl, 145t, 151b
Jo Daley 55r
Dawn Evans 32r, 54l, 54r, 105r, 111l, 119tr, 131tr
Anni Jowlett 101l
Judith Machin 133br
Alison Maddison 103tr
Jacqui Milliken 127l, 137bl
Sarah Mason 11, 64, 65t, 66t, 67t, 68b, 69t, 70t, 71t, 72b, 73t, 101r, 105l, 113t, 115b, 117tl, 119tl, 121t, 125b, 137br, 139tl, 139b, 147t, 147b, 149tr, 151tl, 151tr
Alison McGovern 10, 18, 32l, 91, 103b, 109l, 117b, 123l, 123r, 153tr
Karen McIvor 28, 39t, 39b, 55l, 65b, 67b, 68t, 69b, 70b, 71b, 72t, 73b, 83t, 87tr, 97l, 97r, 99t, 103tl, 107b, 115t, 125t, 127r, 129b, 135b, 139tr, 141t, 143l, 143r, 145b, 149tl, 149b, 153b
Gwyneth Roper 135t
Donna Valance 56t, 111r, 129tl, 133t, 153tl
Mandy Webb 32c, 87tl, 109r, 117tr, 119b, 133bl, 141b

All other photographs and illustrations are the copyright of Quarto Publishing plc. While every effort has been made to credit contributors, Quarto would like to apologise should there have been any omissions or errors – and would be pleased to make the appropriate correction for future editions.

WITH SPECIAL THANKS
Quarto would like to thank the following for their assistance and support:
Meryl Bartho for additional text and images on digital scrapbooking.
Quantum Enterprises (www.quantumenterprises.co.uk) for handwriting fonts.
Digital Scrapbook Place (www.digitalscrapbook place.com) for help on digital scrapbooking.
Anna Griffin Inc (www.annagriffin.com) for decorative background papers used for endpapers.

The following companies supplied materials:
K&Company (www.kandcompany.com)
7 gypsies (www.sevengypsies.com)
Personal Impressions (www.richstamp.co.uk)
Storage 4 Crafts (www.storage4craft.com)
Ellison Design (www.ellisondesign.com)
Stamp Addict (www.stampaddicts.co.uk)
Scrapbook Trade (www.scrapbooktrade.co.uk)
SEI (www.shopsei.com)
Total Papercrafts (www.totalpapercrafts.co.uk)
Scenic Route (www.scenicroutepaper.com)
Stamp Connection (www.thestampconnection.co.uk)